About the Author

Lt. Col. Mary D. Foley USA (Ret.) has been involved with Cockapoos since the early 1980s when she began her All American Cockapoos kennel. With the assistance of fellow Cockapoo lovers, she founded the Cockapoo Club of America, the first organization ever to be dedicated to a designer dog. She holds the title of president emeritus of the club. Currently residing in Florida with Cockapoos, Peaches and Panda, she is shown here with Patches, second generation, and Hercules, ninth generation.

About Our Cover Dog

Meet Mia, a four-year-old Cockapoo, who lives with her adoring owners and caregivers Bob and Mary Buten in Aberdeen, New Jersey. Mia is a sable and white Cockapoo who was bred by Carol Bobrowsky of Mulberry Farm Cockapoos. Mia's favorite activities include playing ball and Frisbee. She loves all people, especially children, and she sleeps in her parents' bed, of course. In her spare time, she eats cheese.

Cockapoo

By Mary D. Foley

The Cockapoo
is a hybrid: the perfect
combination of style,
intelligence and affection.

Kennel Club Books®, the country's only major publisher of exclusively dog books, proudly presents its *Designer Dog Series*™ to celebrate the Cockapoo's coming-out party. Continuing in its bold effort to produce a unique line of dog books, Kennel Club Books® releases the first ever book on the specific designer dog cross-breeds. The company has also released many *Special Limited Editions* and *Special Rare-Breed Editions* on various unusual breeds.

Visit the publisher's website at
www.kennelclubbooks.com
to read more about the unique library of books available to dog lovers around the world.

Acknowledgments

The author wishes to thank the following people for their invaluable help during the production of this book: Dr. Marjorie Rust, for introducing me to her Cockapoo, "Frederick," over 30 years ago and for keeping my old laptop going so I could write the book; Fred Oehme, DVM, Ph.D., Veterinary Toxicologist, Kansas State University, for invaluable assistance with the section on poisonous substances in dogs; Josie Montenari, President, Cockapoo Club of America, who steered the publisher to me and got the ball rolling; Debbie Cowdrey of Starlos kennels, for patiently answering all my questions and providing many wonderful pictures; Jackie Rusk of Camano Island Cockapoos, for her pictures and continued support throughout the project; Jeannie Maruejouls, for taking scads of pictures and helping to sort them; and most of all, all the wonderful people who adopted and loved my Cockapoos when I was breeding, kept in touch over the years and provided me with feedback and encouragement.

KENNEL CLUB BOOKS®
Designer Dog
SERIES™

COCKAPOO
ISBN: 1-59378-591-7

Copyright © 2006 · Kennel Club Books, LLC
308 Main Street, Allenhurst, NJ 07711 USA
Printed in South Korea

Photography by:
Don Ayres, Paulette Braun, Bernd Brinkmann, Debbie Cowdrey, Isabelle Français, Bill Jonas, Jean M. Maruejouls, Jackie Rusk and Karen Taylor.

The publisher would like to thank all of the owners and breeders whose dogs are featured in this book, including Don Ayres, Ken and Patti Bolduc, the Butens, Debbie Cowdrey, Donna Fario, Mary Foley, Monique and Paul Freed, the Gilchrists, the Kimballs, the Kowalskis, Jean M. Maruejouls, Jill McGillam, Kris O'Shaugnessy, Brian and Carol Potter, Patti and Ken Ross, Jackie Rusk, the Satarianos and the Stokes.

10 9 8 7 6 5 4 3 2 1

Contents

The Cocker Spaniel is the dapper daddy of this designer dog.

The font of all "Poos": the Miniature Poodle

History of the
Cockapoo

It is a well-known fact that the
Poodle is among the most intelligent of dogs, probably second
only to the Border Collie. Poodles date back to the Middle
Ages and were used by hunters as waterfowl retrievers
because of their high trainability, superb swimming ability and
buoyant coats and as truffle hunters because of their miraculous
noses. Today Poodles are prized for their intelligence, elegance,
alertness, sociability and grace. They are easy to train to do tricks
and seem almost human at times. One thing not mentioned in
Poodle literature is that they can be extremely good guard dogs.
Thick woolly coats demand frequent brushing in between trips to
the grooming salon. But they are low-shedding and hypoallergenic,
and they do not have doggy odor. (Non-shedding is a misnomer, but
the term low-shedding is more accurate, i.e., hair comes out on the
brush but is not found in any significant quantity around the
house.) Some people groom their own Poodles and spin the wool
into yarn. In the US, the Poodle is divided into three sizes,
Standard, Miniature and Toy; the Miniatures are most frequently
used in Cockapoo crosses.

The Cocker Spaniel was also bred long ago in Europe to hunt
the woodcock, a woodland bird of the sandpiper family. Like
Poodles, Cockers have excellent noses for scenting and they, too, are
great swimmers and retrievers. Cocker Spaniels, by definition, are

is the starting point for the Cockapoo.

Make way, America, for designer dogs—here's the Cockapoo!

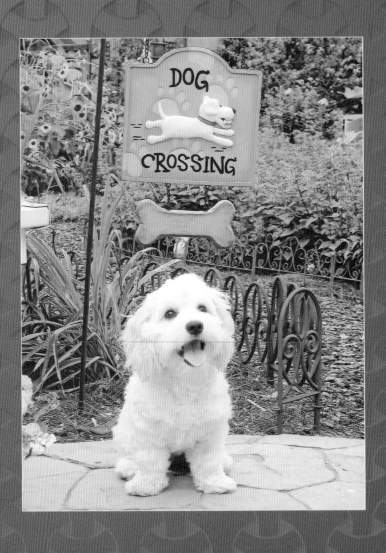

merry little dogs, devoted to their families and with an inherent love of children. They are known to be very intelligent and quick learners. Their coats are extremely thick, particularly on the legs, ears and chest, and grooming, as in the Poodle, is very demanding. Unlike the Poodle, the Cocker sheds profusely and tends to have some doggy odor. Throughout the world, there are two breeds of Cocker, the American Cocker, the more popular in the US, more profusely coated breed, and the English Cocker, less common in the US but very popular in the UK.

Both the Poodle and Cocker have been high in popularity for many years and have been bred by American breeders to develop "beautiful show dogs," sometimes to the detriment of health and temperament. Some poorly bred Poodles are infamous for their high-strung behavior and constant barking. Some American Cockers have also become nervous and high-strung and prone to rage syndrome and skin disorders. Each breed, because of inferior breeding practices and mass production by profit-minded kennels, is prone to many genetic diseases. Heritable eye disease in both breeds is one of the most prominent, leading to early cataracts, glaucoma and blindness.

This author's experience with the Cockapoo dates back to 1974 when she met a friend's Cockapoo in Colorado. At that time, the author had a small black Standard Poodle. In 1982, when the author was nearing retirement from the US Army Nurse Corps and again stationed in Colorado, the Poodle died of kidney failure at the impressive age of 16 and a half years of age. Meanwhile, the next-door neighbors had a small black shaggy dog that they said was a Cockapoo, who was bred to an apricot Miniature Poodle. The puppies were adorable! And after weeks of playing with them, an apricot female wormed her way into my heart. In raising her, she seemed to learn everything by osmosis. She had perfect manners, was naturally house-trained and never chewed

COCKAPOOS IN PRINT

There are very few references to Cockapoos in dog books even to this day. The author has encountered only two. In *The New Encyclopedia of the Dog*, second edition, by Brian Fogle, DVM, one-quarter of a page in this beautifully bound hardbound book is devoted to what Fogel calls a "Cockerpoo." The book states that the country of origin is the US and the date of origin is the 1960s. Its use is as a companion dog, life expectancy 13–15 years, weight 20–24 pounds, height 14–15 inches. He states, "The Cockerpoo is now so common that it may soon have breed standards and formal recognition"[by the AKC]. The book provides a beautiful picture of a large apricot-colored Cockerpoo and provides some general physical standards. He describes temperament as: "the Cockerpoo is an intent observer, not given to the hyperactive excesses of many American Cocker Spaniels. An added feature is that the Cockerpoo has a much lower incidence of skin problems than the American Cocker." The physical standard that Dr. Fogle suggests is: "Prominent ridge on skull, as in the Cocker Spaniel, ample jaws, well spaced teeth, sturdy back as long as is high. Face resembles both Cocker and Poodle; dense coat protects skin, tail long and close." He further states, "hip joints do not suffer inherited problems, hereditary slack kneecaps seldom occur."

The other is a very short reference in a British book entitled *Dog, The Complete Guide* by Sarah Whitehead, copyright 1999: "for example, the Cockerpoo and the Pekepoo, in which Poodles have been crossed with other breeds, have now become so popular that it is likely they will soon be recognized as new breeds. The Markiesje (Toy Poodle crossed with Continental Spaniels) is now officially recognized by the Dutch Kennel Club."

anything inappropriate. She always was dying to please. Her name was Ginger, but I called her Ginger Goody Twoshoes, because she was perfect, so smart, personable, friendly and willing to please. Although her coat was easy to care for, it possessed those desirable Poodle coat qualities of being low-shedding and clean-smelling. Ginger was bred to an unrelated Cockapoo in the neighborhood, and the seeds of All American Cockapoos were sown. The pups were sold to friends or colleagues for $50, only after serious inquiry into their ability to care for the pups. Word got back from one couple that they "did not face that much scrutiny when they adopted their son."

Following a post-retirement move to Santa Rosa, California, the search for a Cockapoo breeder began. It took 6 months to find Bette H., who by that time had been seriously breeding Cockapoos for about 30 years. She had lovely tempered, healthy dogs that looked more Poodle than Cocker because that is the look she liked. Remember that there were no standards, so each breeder did her "own thing." Bette had been an

American Kennel Club (AKC) Poodle breeder who also owned AKC Cockers.

By the time we met, she bred only Cockapoo to Cockapoo and no longer had the parental breeds. She developed unrelated lines of various sizes and bred down through the generations using only unrelated pairs. Bette was a woman of high integrity and energy who really loved her dogs, kept them and their quarters immaculate, was careful about selecting owners and followed up on the pups. One knew that Bette's dogs were pure Cockapoos as stated, with no other breed mixed in. She sold her dogs for $500 and up in 1985.

Thus began many years of friendship and collegiality. In further developing All American Cockapoos, Cockapoo stock was purchased from Bette and other breeders (none the stature of Bette's). The original business plan for All American Cockapoos was to acquire high-quality AKC Poodles and Cockers and crossbreed them down the generations. In searching for AKC breeders to obtain stock, their rudeness was almost universal, amounting to, "How dare anyone try to create a new breed or breed a mutt?" By definition, the Cockapoo is a hybrid, not a mutt. A mutt (or the old-

WHAT'S IN A NAME?

The Cockapoo, also referred to as Cockerpoo and Cock-a-poo, is not a breed but is a hybrid cross of equal parts Cocker Spaniel and Poodle. Rarely, breeders have used the English Cocker Spaniel in the crosses, and these dogs are known as English Cockapoos. The name "Cockapoo" seems to be the one in most common usage. There are also a few breeders crossing Springer Spaniels with Standard Poodles to create very large dogs for use on farms.

It is difficult to determine how long ago or why the Cocker Spaniel and Poodle breeds were crossed in the first place. Most likely it has been done as long as the parental breeds have existed. But it seems like they really caught on in the US around the 1960s. There is evidence of Cockapoos in France toward the turn of the 20th century. Germany now has its own Cockapoo club (patterned after the American parent club, the Cockapoo Club of America) and so does Australia, where the hybrid is called a Spoodle.

A black Cocker Spaniel can be solid colored or with tan points, like this handsome example.

fashioned term "cur") is a dog of unknown parentage, the good old "Heinz 57." This judgmental attitude proved to be pervasive among AKC breeders and judges of that day. They did not seem to realize that all of today's recognized breeds were once "mutts."

The brazen condescension even extended to insulting Cockapoos and those who bred them in various forums, including, eventually, on the Internet. Well-known AKC judges went so far as to accuse all Cockapoo breeders of being puppy mills.

It is important, at this point, for us to differentiate between these prejudicial AKC breeders and judges and the American Kennel Club itself. Over the years, individuals called upon at AKC headquarters have been courteous, helpful and non-judgmental. One gentleman in the registry knew of a woman in Tucson who had been breeding Cockapoos for 40 years. He even checked on this for me, but the woman had died and all records were lost.

And so, not being able to find any support in the pure-bred dog community, and

A Miniature Poodle stands over 10 and up to 15 inches at the shoulder.

being a goal-oriented, medical model, scientific Type A personality, I devoted most of my energy to becoming the best read, most responsible Cockapoo breeder possible. In a way, the AKC community did me a favor, as the pure-bred dog community is loaded with more unscientific, unfounded "old wives' tales" than you can imagine. Nurses are inveterate record keepers and so, even though not actively breeding anymore, my records go back to the first pup I ever sold.

Bette continued to be my only mentor, as I found that, in acquiring Cockapoo stock, most were family operations led by novice breeders. During travels to find Cockapoo stock, I encountered many fraudulent breeders whose dogs were anything but Cocker and Poodle stock, but who were cunning enough to know that Cockapoos sold quickly and advertised any kind of pup as such. This was so rampant in Washington State and Arizona that fraudulent breeders were reported to the local animal control, the courts and even the newspapers.

The Poodle today is being crossed with many different breeds because of its intelligence and the fact that the low-shedding, odorless coat seems to be a dominant trait passed on in the first generation to all puppies, no matter with which breed they are crossed. This low-shed quality is very much in demand and a prime considera-tion for many people in today's society where dogs are a part of the family, are kept indoors, sleep in owners' beds and are taken many places in the family car. The popularity of all of the "Poo" crosses is beyond belief, and these Peekapoos, Labradoodles, Pomapoos, Schnoodles, Pugapoos and other "Poo" dogs are being bred by an assortment of people. These designer dogs usually sell for tidy sums with no background genetic testing and no guaran-tees, pedigrees or AKC papers on the parental breeds. There does not seem to be any major effort to form breed clubs for these other Poodle-crossed dogs or to breed down the generations. The one exception, besides the Cockapoo, is the Labradoodle.

The author attributes the recent popularity of the Poodle crosses to all of the publicity in the 1990s that pointed out the sadly compromised state of the congenital/hereditary health of pure-bred dogs in America. An article entitled "A Terrible Beauty" by Michael D. Lemonick, in the December 12, 1994 issue of *Time* magazine, reported that, "An obsessive focus on show-ring looks is crippling, sometimes fatally, America's pure-bred dogs." The article points out the many genetic defects in pure-bred dogs and the AKC's unwillingness to do anything about it. In 1992, investigative journalist Larry Shook wrote a book called *The Puppy Report*, "an indispensable guide to finding a healthy lovable pet." He explores and exposes commercial breeding establishments that are breeding and registering AKC dogs and is critical of the AKC for not doing more about this tragedy. Since those publications were written, the AKC has done a lot to evaluate kennels and write guidelines for kennels and breeders. And now many breed

Enter the Labradoodle

The original Labrador Retriever-Poodle cross was done purposely in Australia in order to provide a non-allergenic guide dog for a blind woman in Hawaii. One primary breeder seems to be Beverley Manners of the Rutland Manor Breeding and Research Center in Australia. Beverley has a nice website at www.rutlandmanor.com. As with the Cockapoo, the Labradoodle has caught on and is being bred all over America. These dogs seem to sell for prices comparable to those for top-quality AKC breeds. Rutland Manor is unique in that it uses only outcross (mating only non-related pairs) breeding down to the sixth generation.

clubs are recommending genetic testing of breeding stock.

As a result of Shook's book and features in *Time* and on television, the public became more aware of the problems in pure-bred dogs and started looking toward rescuing mutts from shelters instead of purchasing puppies from AKC breeders. This publicity also hurt the AKC, which at this point had done little about the fraudulent activities of breeders. Fortunately, the American Kennel Club has implemented kennel inspection programs, DNA testing and many checks and balances to attempt to see that the dogs they register are indeed pure-bred.

Let's consider now why this cute-as-a-button hybrid pooch, the Cockapoo, has become so popular that existing breeders cannot meet the demand. As we've mentioned, any breed crossed with a Poodle is very popular today. There are Lhasapoos, Shihpoos, Chihuapoos, Pomapoos, Schnoodles, Peekapoos, Bi-poos (Bichon/Poodle), Yorkiepoos and, of course, the up-and-coming Labradoodles. They are all cute furry bundles, and many believe them to be improvements on the parental breeds, possessing fewer genetic defects and the well-known sound temperaments and hybrid vigor of the traditional mutt.

This dashing designer dog is a Dachsiepoo, a hybrid Miniature Poodle and Standard Dachshund.

Who could resist the charms of this "Golden Bundle" of "Poo" wonder?

The mellow attitude
of the Cocker Spaniel
and the intelligence of the Poodle...

Characteristics of the
Cockapoo

The Cockapoo inherited from the Poodle its extraordinary intelligence and its non-shedding coat. Happily, there is very little dander, which is the main culprit in causing people's allergies to dogs. From the Cocker comes a sweet and patient nature, a calm and mellow disposition, a natural affinity for children and a sturdy build. This type of crossbreeding usually results in "hybrid vigor" in which the best qualities of each breed are manifested in the offspring. The former statement presupposes that breeders are using only high-quality Cockers and Poodles with the soundest dispositions and clear health/genetic testing. Crossbreeding also creates a wider genetic pool and lessens the likelihood of the more prominent defects of each breed being reproduced. This, however, does not apply to genetic defects common to both breeds. Continued outcrossing (breeding unrelated pairs) enlarges the gene pool even further.

The personality of the Cockapoo is unparalleled in its affection for people. Cockapoos are loyal, open and friendly. They are most receptive to young people and highly regarded for being extremely tolerant of children's clumsy handling. Cockapoos generally are non-destructive around the house and clean. They are eager to please and therefore easily trained. Health-wise, they can hardly be beat as they remain vigorous and active for most of their years; some dogs live to be 15 to 22 years of age.

still don't rule out a little mischief here and there!

IMPORTANCE OF HEALTH CLEARANCES

Regardless if you are buying a dog of pure-bred or mixed-breed heritage, it is important to see the parents' health clearances. Parents with good hearts, eyes clear of cataracts and well-structured hips will help the pup's buyer feel better about the overall health of the puppy he intends to purchase.

Be certain to request viewing the Orthopedic Foundation for Animals (OFA) and Canine Eye Registration Foundation (CERF) certifications on both parents. The hips should be tested as Fair, Good or Excellent. The eyes must be cataract-free and free from other common canine genetic problems, and the heart strong and healthy. Never purchase a puppy from a breeder without having seen the parents' clearances!

As most mixed-breed dogs are obtained through shelters, humane societies and rescue groups, you will almost never have the opportunity to view, or even know, anything about the parents. Be aware, however, that many mixed breeds can be healthier than many pure-breds, as one parent can counterbalance the recessive genes for disease in the other parent.

COCKAPOO CLUBS

The author founded the Cockapoo Club of America (CCA) in 1998; the goal of this parent club is to protect, preserve and gain respectability within the dog fancy for the Cockapoo. Furthermore, the CCA seeks to promote genetic testing and breeding down the generations, eventually gaining breed status. The author and several prominent breeders developed a "breed" standard for the Cockapoo, including the physical traits (size, head, general appearance) and temperament. The Cockapoo Club of America is a non-profit, educational corporation with bylaws and a board of directors. There is a wealth of information on the website at www.cockapooclub.com, covering all aspects of breeding, puppy raising and business tips and forms. The major departure from most pure-bred parent clubs is the CCA's emphasis that health and temperament should remain foremost and take priority over physical type. It is anticipated that as the Cockapoo Club of America and the Cockapoo itself develop further toward becoming a real breed, physical standards can become more specific.

Another organization dedicated to the Cockapoo is the North American Cockapoo Registry (NACR), a private business founded by Lucille Bailey as a registry for Cockapoos. It also has a breed standard, which the author feels dovetails with that of the CCA. To read the NACR's breed standard, go to its website: http://www.cockapoos.com and look under "General Info." The NACR, by its own statement, is strictly a registry and takes no responsibility for the quality of the breeders registering with them. It is the most viable of the registries currently available for the Cockapoo.

THE TAO OF "POO"

Poodles are one of the oldest breeds of dog in the world. Originally bred in Europe as hunting dogs, they quickly gained fame in France as circus performers. Poodles are intelligent, enjoying long lifespans and dirt-resistant, water-repellent coats. They come in three recognized sizes and myriad solid colors ranging from white to black and everything in between. Poodles are one of the few breeds considered hypoallergenic due to a low shedding rate. It is their coats that made them popular in the recent designer dog craze, but it is their intelligence and temperaments that truly enhance the outcome.

Second-generation apricots owned by the author. They have characteristic appealing furry faces and deep, brown, healthy eyes.

REGISTRY

The Cockapoo Club of America plans to develop its own registry in the near future. In the meantime, keep very accurate records and keep any papers on your dogs.

THE ORIGINAL STANDARD FOR THE COCKAPOO AS ADOPTED BY THE COCKAPOO CLUB OF AMERICA

General: A dog that does not look like either of the originating parental breeds and yet incorporates the features of both. Unclipped has the general and appealing "Benji" appearance. Most prominent are large, brown, intelligent looking eyes on a captivating furry face.

Tail: Undocked, carried straight or curled.

Eyes: Large, round, well-set brown eyes with a keen, soulful, endearing and intelligent look. Hair should be scissored back so as not to obstruct the eyes or vision. All breeding dogs should be examined annually by a veterinary ophthalmologist and certified by the Canine Eye Registration Foundation (CERF) to be free of genetic eye disease.

Ears: Medium to long, not erect but hanging down.

Dewclaws: Removed for safety purposes.

Conformation: A sturdy square build with a healthy back structure; compact, well balanced, neither spindly nor coarse.

Bite: Aligned scissors bite with neither over- nor underbite.

Colors: All colors and combinations are acceptable.

Coat: Long and full all over including legs and muzzle. Can be loose curly, wavy to straight, but not kinky. Long, natural, well-groomed coats are preferred. Otherwise they may be scissored to about 1–3 inches, depending on size.

Size Ranges: Pounds are used as a criteria instead of the more traditional inches as variations in build can be expected until such time as the Cockapoo breeds true.

Teacup Toy: Under 6 pounds grown weight.

Toy: 7–12 pounds.

Miniature: 13–18 pounds.

Maxi: Over 19 pounds.

Disqualifications: Dogs with these traits should not be bred: aggressiveness, shyness, poor health, genetic disease history and uncertain parentage.

Shows

The development of any breed has been delineated by its shows and judging. This is a tried and true way to encourage breeders to breed as close to the breed standard as possible. Hopefully, when there are Cockapoo shows in the future, there will be a departure from the current AKC shows in that they might be more low key, more informal, fun and less stressful. The accent will be on health, genetic testing and temperament, perhaps 75% on temperament and 25% on physical standards.

Dog shows can be great fun for the dogs and all members of the family. Picture yourself and your dog on a large grassy field with colorful tents, rings and vendors selling dog-related items and food. There are many families and their beloved Cockapoos, all wandering about, comparing their dogs and having fun.

Unlike AKC shows where one judge determines the winner in the class, Cockapoo shows would be judged by a panel of judges, perhaps three, each doing his own scoring on each dog. Scores would be combined to determine placements and winners. There would be areas where a panel of judges could test and evaluate the dogs' temperaments, personalities, responsiveness and showmanship. Ideally, the judges would be seated on the floor or a bench in informal attire to interact with each dog. There would also be children of various ages present as stewards for the judges.

Each dog would also have to be exposed to other dogs to assess his degree of friendliness. Does the dog greet other dogs with a wagging tail or a growl? Any signs of aggression toward people or other dogs would be cause for dismissal. Likewise, any signs of cruelty or unnatural altering done to a dog to enhance his chances of winning would disqualify the dog from the show.

After passing the temperament tests and obtaining their scores, the Cockapoos would go to rings to again be judged by a panel on how close they come to the physical standard. From this point on, the show becomes more like conventional shows. As many dogs as possible would win ribbons or trophies in some category.

Starlo's Bambi is a first-generation Cockapoo bred by the author.

COCKAPOO SHOWS IN THE FUTURE

The author certainly has her own views about what Cockapoo shows of the future should be like. Indulge her, if you will. First there would be pre-registration for various classes: whole (meaning sexually intact) males and whole females by size, whose categories would have very strict demands as to pedigrees and genetic testing. These classes are the core of dogs competing to produce the show dogs of the future. All dogs would be required to have a health certificate from a veterinarian and verification of current shots. There would also be categories to include spayed and neutered pets, with and without pedigree papers, puppy classes, obedience, flyball, doggie dancing and other fun competitions!

GENETICS AND HEALTH CONCERNS

Articles in *Time* and *The Atlantic Monthly* brought into the public eye many of the negative aspects of the genetic health of pure-bred dogs. Many believe that the reason for so many hereditary conditions in pure-bred dogs lies in the inbreeding and line-breeding done to set traits for the show ring. For the most part, the breeds that are the most popular have the most hereditary problems. This stands to reason as these breeds attract the profit-seeking breeders, who are not concerned with health problems and only breed for financial gain. Some breeders tend to be in denial or be the proverbial ostrich with its head in the sand as far as genetic flaws in their dogs. The breed clubs and the AKC dragged their feet on the issue for many years. Still, the vast majority of breeders, if asked about the prominent genetic

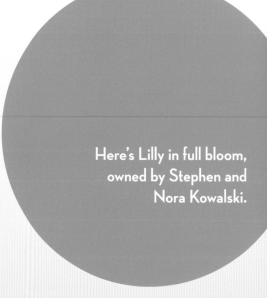

Here's Lilly in full bloom, owned by Stephen and Nora Kowalski.

problems in their breed, will say that there are none (or very few) in their dogs.

Unfortunately, both of the Cockapoo's auspicious progenitors are loaded with genetic defects. The American Cocker and the Poodle run about midway in the lists of genetic defects for all breeds. For instance, say the German Shepherd, one of the worst breeds from a hereditary-disease point of view, has 80+ defects listed, the American Cocker and the Poodle have somewhere around 40 to 50 each and at the bottom of the list are breeds such as the Cardigan Welsh Corgi and the Parson Russell Terrier, with about 4 each. Does the Parson Russell Terrier's low incidence have anything to do with the fact that inbreeding and line-breeding have been discouraged by the clubs for years?

Luckily, some of the "ostriches" are finally lifting their sandy heads to see the light. If one searches the Internet, breed clubs have begun to address the issues and educate their members. For example, the American Spaniel Club, the parent club for the Cocker, has an excellent website (www.asc-cocker spaniel.org) addressing health problems and also has certification programs for eyes, thyroid and a host of other problems.

Some of the more prominent and major genetic defects common to both the Poodle and Cocker include progressive retinal atrophy (PRA) and other serious heritable eye diseases, epilepsy, cartilage and bone

problems, luxating patellas in the Toy Poodle, tumors and skin problems. Of course, the Cockapoo is not immune to genetic defects. Probably the most prominent defect in both Poodles and Cockers today, PRA results in early blindness and painful glaucoma. Depending on the dog and the disease, blindness can occur as early as 3 to 6 years of age, or later, by around age 15 years. The only thing that an owner can do is submit the dog to expensive care by a veterinary ophthalmologist to attempt to control the glaucoma.

For years, the author has been recommending that all breeding stock obtain yearly eye exams by a certified veterinary ophthalmologist. The CCA also recommends these clearances. The findings are reported to the Canine Eye Registration Foundation (CERF), so the exam is called a CERF exam. CERF maintains a database of dogs by breed and the results of their eye exams. The CCA was responsible for having CERF add the Cockapoo as one of its "breeds." Sadly, the ones who do not pass their eye exams are rarely reported, thus distorting statistics for the breeders who care.

Heritable eye disease is so prominent that a Poodle or Cocker breeder may lose up to half his stock on a first exam. So one can see why the vast majority of breeders continue to hide their heads in the sand and claim the problem does not exist in their stock! It takes a brave kennel owner/breeder to face this possibility, and one with the highest integrity to admit it. Some use the cost of the exams as an excuse, but it is usually only a moderate price for the first dog, and most veterinary ophthalmologists give multiple-dog discounts. The best excuse I read on a breeder's website was: "No, we don't CERF because you can CERF one day and the dog can get a detached retina the next." CERF exams are not about detached retinas!

Ophthalmologists will often come to a kennel to do the screening. Even so, CERF is not a perfect solution, as the eye exam may be clear at two years of age before the dog is bred, and then the same dog fails the exam later after having produced several litters. Puppies can be checked as early as eight weeks, though follow-ups are necessary to screen for clearance. The CERF exam checks for dogs with active disease; it cannot detect recessive genes. Again, two disease-free dogs carrying recessive genes may produce dogs with active disease. There is an excellent website covering canine eye genetics for readers interested in more details: www.eyevet.org. Until DNA testing in dogs becomes widely available and reasonably priced, CERF is the best avenue we have.

These are the reasons that the Cockapoo Club of America led the way, by educating Cockapoo breeders to perform health testing and owners to demand that all possible genetic testing be done on breeder stock. Hip dysplasia is not a significant problem in either breed, but patellar luxation is a problem in small breeds including Poodles, and elbow dysplasia is prominent in the Cocker. There are tests and certifications available from the Orthopedic Foundation for Animals (OFA) for these problems. Visit its website at www.offa.org.

NAKED COCKAPOO ALERT

The coat should be wavy or slightly curly and does require a minimum of twice-weekly brushing or combing to prevent mats and occasional baths for cleanliness. The Cockapoo, left untrimmed, except for trimming around eyes and genitals, and subjected to daily combing, is a beauty to behold but is rarely seen. Also very attractive are Cockapoos who are scissored to a length of 1 to 3 inches, depending on the dog's height. Least attractive and most common are Cockapoos who never see a brush or comb between dates with the groomer and are shaved very close to the skin. The author calls these "naked Cockapoos." Don't be caught with a naked Cockapoo—take care of his coat and make him look proud and handsome.

The Cockapoo exudes a joy for li

Is a Cockapoo Right for You?

A Cockapoo is designed and bred to be a family dog that has a superior ability to relate to both children and adults. With his unique intelligence and eagerness to please, there is not much that a Cockapoo could not be trained to do. He could be trained in search and rescue, as a guide dog for the blind or hearing dog for the deaf, as an assistance dog for the physically disabled and even as a performance dog in obedience, agility, flyball, tracking and retrieving. Nonetheless, the Cockapoo's primary function is as a companion dog.

He becomes very attached to his owner and if allowed, no matter what the size, would be a lapdog. Although there are many stories of Cockapoos herding children away from danger and protecting their families, they are not bred to be guard dogs. If you want a dog for protection and guardwork, then you best look at other breeds. The Cockapoo's face alone would melt the heart of the most hardened criminal and could easily make friends.

CONSIDERING THE COCKAPOO

The biggest drawback to the Cockapoo is the attention needed for the coat. He will love to go anywhere with his person or family, but treks through the woods or on trails will require a great deal of grooming afterwards to remove burrs and ticks from the coat. A prospective owner needs to consider not only his current lifestyle but also his future prospects in choosing the dog that is right for him. For

nd exuberance that are hard to resist.

instance, a single person may not consider children in his "lifestyle snapshot" when he's choosing a dog. In a short year or two, he could be married with twins! You never want to re-home a dog, if at all possible. This is a very painful thing for owner and dog, especially the affectionate Cockapoo, so why not think ahead? Adopting a dog represents a commitment for the life of the dog. In the case of a Cockapoo, that could be around 20 years.

Also consider what you have to offer a Cockapoo. Is a fenced yard a must? Not necessarily, but walking the dog at least three times a day so that he can relieve himself is a must. Many people with fenced yards use doggie doors so that the pet can let himself in and out at will, but consider what the dog will be doing when he is out without your supervision. Lonely dogs tend to bark, dig, climb the drapes and eat houseplants, and barking and running away will not make your neighbors your friends. Some of these behaviors are dangerous to the dog; at the very least, your local animal control officer will not be amused by your defiant Cockapoo. You must consider the safety of your Cockapoo, as larger dogs could even jump the fence and attack your smaller dog.

The Cockapoo is not an outdoor dog to be left alone 14 hours a day while you are at work. The Cockapoo does not need constant companionship by any means; this, in fact, would not be good for any dog, but he does need attention. Do not get a dog because you are lonely for human companionship. Get a dog when you feel that you really have something to offer the dog in the way of time, training, the right living situation and funds available to properly care for him.

Funds are a big considera-tion along with time to spend with the pet. In addition to the initial cost of the puppy, which will be quite expensive for certain, there are food, toys, grooming tools and salon visits, obedience classes and, of course, veterinary costs. Many owners also invest in doggie daycare, which is a terrific idea two or

The Cockapoo is an intelligent, curious dog who will have plenty of exploring to do, so you must provide him with a safe area to play and careful supervision.

RECOGNIZING A KNOWLEDGEABLE BREEDER

Ever walk into a kennel and want to hold your nose? Or walk into someone's backyard where there are "dog piles" everywhere or rusty, old dog runs filled with puppies playing in their own messes? As much as you feel sorry for these puppies, you can be certain that they have not been bred by a knowledgeable breeder. This is not a breeder who should be getting designer-dog prices for his poorly bred and raised puppies. However, these conditions should be reported to the appropriate authorities for the sake of the resident pups' (and their parents') welfare.

A knowledgeable breeder will maintain a clean, healthy environment for all dogs and puppies. The puppies will be socialized from an early age, receiving the attention and handling they need from the breeder. The puppies will also have received appropriate worming treatments and vaccinations prior to being allowed to leave the breeder's premises. A responsible breeder will also make sure that his puppies go to good homes. Be ready to be scrutinized prior to being allowed to purchase a pup.

ALLURE OF DESIGNER DOGS

Poodle mixes are quickly gaining in popularity, even though many pure-bred dog breeders continue to "poo-poo" the Poodle crosses. Nevertheless, the allure of the designer dog has captivated thousands of people, and fortunately there are many dedicated breeders producing healthy, sound and lovely Cockapoos to meet the demand for these undeniably terrific dogs.

Each puppy is unique and offers the benefits of the Poodle heritage: intelligence, an easy-care coat and a nice temperament. The more that people seek out these mixes, the more that breeders will produce them. One must watch out for poorly bred pups, though, as unscrupulous breeders will eagerly mix their breeding stock to fulfill the high demand. The designer-dog purchaser needs to be just as careful when purchasing his Poodle cross as he would be if purchasing a pure-bred.

equal a month's salary (unless you're a vet or a doctor yourself!). Are you prepared to cover this sort of expenditure? A wise modern option is veterinary insurance, which could save your dog's life (and your bank account) in the face of an accident or a devastating illness.

These are just things to consider when thinking of getting a dog, and by no means does the author mean to imply that only wealthy people should have dogs. Make sound decisions based on your lifestyle and income, not upon your crush on the irresistible Cockapoo. Sadly, the vast majority of people buy pets on impulse, making purely emotional decisions because of their own neediness or because they are emotional buyers. A puppy is not something you can return if you discover you don't like the color or size!

Coincidentally, the Cockapoo comes in different sizes, just like blouses and T-shirts, essentially small, medium or large. If you have children, consider whether

three times a week if you work full-time. Consider kennel costs as well if you plan to board your dog when you go on vacation. Take the time to call and see what a vet charges for the basic series of shots and exams, heartworm blood tests and medication. If your pet gets ill or has an accident, it would not be uncommon to run up vet bills to

they are rough-and-tumble kids or the rarer gentle, more serious, ones. For most active families, the medium or larger Cockapoo better fits the bill; for singles or older adults, the tiny ones may be appropriate. Tiny ones should never go to homes with active small children. Never let your children choose the pup; you are the parent. Make your choice using recommendations from the breeder.

We Americans, as a society, seem to be a people used to instant gratification. The demand for Cockapoos far outstrips the availability, and good breeders have long waiting lists. The fussier you are about color, sex and size, the longer you may wait. Yet, it is worth the wait to get a dog from a good breeder. And good breeders love thoughtful families who have done their research. When the author was breeding, she was often heard to say, "I wish all the children in the world could be born to the types of families who have my dogs."

The Potter family includes Cockapoos Gretchen and Megan.

Are you ready to welcome a Cockapoo

The Cockapoo Club of

America (CCA) (www.cockapooclub.com) has a list of breeders all over the US and Canada and makes a good attempt to assess breeder quality by site visits and feedback from clients. There is a nominal charge for the breeder list but you can get to talk to or email a live person with your questions and comments. The CCA does not have a registry of its own.

You can also search the Internet to look for a breeder in your location. Do not be "sold" on the breeder simply by the super-jazziness of a website. You're shopping for a puppy breeder, not a webmaster. Some of the worst breeders have the most amazing websites! Do not ever order a puppy over the Internet from a breeder you do not know. If nothing else, ask for references and phone numbers of at least three people who have their dogs.

The North American Cockapoo Registry (NACR) also has a list of breeders on its website. Remember that the NACR is an excellent registry but does not bear any responsibility for the quality of the breeders they list. They list only those breeders who register their dogs with them. They do have a breed standard and other good advice for the consumer. This is the best registry of all those available that is specifically oriented to the advancement of the Cockapoo.

into your home, your heart and your life?

Okay, so you have considered all of the above and want to begin your search for a good breeder. What do you look for? Your first step will be to contact a breeder either by phone (preferred) or by email. Is the breeder caring and sympathetic to your needs? Do the answers to your questions reflect those of a knowledgeable person or are they evasive? When you ask the all-important questions about genetic faults in his dogs, is he honest or does he slough you off with vague disclaimers. Ask how long he has been breeding, about the temperament and health of the parents and if the pups are traceable to American Kennel Club (AKC) Cocker and Poodle lines.

The breeder should be interested in learning about the type of home you can provide, your history with pets, your familiarity with Cockapoos, ages of children, etc. Does he show any

A handful of love, ready to go home.

interest in you and what you have to offer one of his puppies? Last should be a discussion about costs of puppies.

The initial cost of a puppy from a breeder who can prove AKC backgrounds (thus relatively assuring that you are really getting a Cockapoo), who breeds to the standard, whose stock has been certified by CERF for eyes and by the OFA for patellar luxation, elbows and hips and who is breeding down the generations will be much higher than from a breeder who sells just "plain ole Cockerpoos." The higher cost should reflect the cost of genetically tested parents, written warranties for health and temperament and a written sales contract that specifies your options if there is a problem later on. Even though the old maxim is true, "you get what you pay for," in this day of designer dogs, even average Cockapoos can

SHELTER MY IMAGINATION

There are more pure-breds and mixed-breed dogs at animal shelters than you can imagine. Visiting a shelter will both break your heart and open you up to the love of a dog. Most of the canine residents are adults, and few will find homes in time to save their lives.

Most busy households simply do not have the time to house-train a puppy. Obtaining an adult dog from the shelter becomes a great option, as dogs over the age of six months can contain themselves longer than a pup, thus possibly being easier to house-train. Some adult dogs who have been turned over to shelters by their owners may already be house-trained. Many older dogs merely need a warm rug or foot to lie upon and are less demanding companions than the high-energy puppy who is always on the go.

Imagine the life that you can save and enjoy when obtaining an adult dog from a shelter.

A three-week-old
fourth-generation
litter bred by the
author, learning to eat
solid food.

LIFESTYLE CHOICES

Dogs are often chosen to fill the gaps in our fast-paced lives. Americans are having children later in life or sometimes not having any at all. Dogs are fulfilling the need to have "someone" to nurture. Just as the allure of designer clothing grabs our attention, the ability to own a unique or rare breed of dog has become a symbol of success.

However, as many people are becoming aware, dogs are not pieces of furniture to just sit in a room and look nice, nor are they clothing that can be put away in the closet when you no longer wish to wear it. Dogs need attention, care and training. They require much of their human companions' time, especially those dogs that have the blood of high-activity breeds running through their veins.

Designer dogs are becoming more prominent at animal shelters and rescue groups, without the high price tags, as those people with busy lifestyles who wanted canine status symbols are throwing the dogs away just as they would discard items of clothing that are taking up space in the dresser.

be expensive. If possible, you will want to choose a breeder within reasonable driving distance so that you can make multiple visits to meet him, the sire and dam and the litter. Nonetheless, rather than get a local dog of inferior quality from a disreputable breeder, it is better to deal with a highly reputable one and have the puppy shipped.

There are many individuals (who call themselves "breeders") selling any little mixed breed as a Cockapoo because they are capitalizing on the fact that Cockapoos are so popular and relatively hard to find. Don't let the designer-dog craze set the tone of your purchase. The better the breeder, the better the warranty and the health and temperament checks will be. Be sure you get what you are paying for. There is no such thing as a bargain puppy. You will easily spend five times the bargain price every year at the vet's office trying to keep your beloved little runt in reasonable health. Pay the price a responsible breeder demands

and watch your veterinarian starve! For the first ten years of your Cockapoo's life, you should not spend any more at the vet's than ordinary maintenance expenses. So, in reality, your "bargain" pup may wind up costing a small fortune (in dollars and heartaches) and you may or may not wind up with a healthy and temperamentally sound pup.

In addition to the impression of the breeder that you garnered over the phone or email, you can check a breeder out with the local humane society. If your suspicions are raised, do not deal with him, even if it is convenient travel-wise. If all is going well at this point, the next step will be a visit to the breeder with your family (even if there are not any puppies for sale at this time). Sometimes this is not geographically feasible, in which case you need to rely on your gut feelings, obtaining and checking references from people who own the breeder's pups, and the reputation of the breeder.

VISITING THE BREEDER

The visit is a chance for you to see the environmental and social conditions under which the puppies are raised. It is also a chance for the breeder to get to know you and your children (if any). Meeting the dam and hopefully the sire is mandatory, and we don't mean looking at a dog in a crate or kennel run. Pups and parents should be friendly but not overbearing or hyper, shy or depressed. They should be relatively clean and free of sores, look and act healthy and be responsive and vital. Take note of all of the dogs' temperaments—are they extroverted, friendly and easily approachable? If you do not like the parents, you are highly unlikely to get a satisfactory pup out of them. You should be allowed to see all places on the premises where puppies are raised and dogs kept, and ask to see papers proving American Kennel Club backgrounds and CERF and OFA clearances. Even in a kennel situation, there should be a place where the breeder can sit down with the prospective owners of his pups.

Temperament in Cockapoos must be seriously considered before deciding on a breeder and his stock. Remember that some Cockers have a reputation for nasty and aggressive dispositions. Poodles have a reputation for neurotic and hyper behaviors. Some years ago, a woman came to me to have her Cockapoo bred. While assessing where she got the dog and asking if she had met the parents, she said, "Oh, no, they were biters and the woman had to lock them up." She had a little tiny girl with her and admitted the dog had bitten her several times "but never broke the skin." Of course, I refused to breed the dog and gave the owner quite a lecture on the irresponsibility of having a dog like that around a small child. She left weeping because, of course, she loved the dog in spite of her problems, the way mothers do. Nowadays, there are some trainers with expertise in changing fear biting and aggressive behavior.

A first-generation Cockapoo litter at six weeks of age, bred by Starlos kennel. What a colorful clan!

PURCHASING A COCKAPOO

Most breeders release pups to new homes no sooner than six weeks of age and do not ship in air cargo sooner than ten weeks. Pups have a fear period between eight and ten weeks in which frightening experiences can imprint and emotionally damage the pup. At the time that you pick up your puppy, you should have in hand the sales contract, pedigree papers, written instructions on the care and feeding of your puppy and also a crate and bedding. Hopefully you have all of these things before you pick up your new Cockapoo pup.

An ideal sales contract will give you at least four to seven days to get the pup to your vet to be checked over and will cover the replacement cost of the pup and vet bills if the pup develops an illness that can be traced back to the breeder. This contract should also guarantee the pup to be free of genetic defects for at least a year. The contract must be specific as to the type of defects covered. For example, if you buy a male puppy as a pet and not for breeding, something like an

HYPOALLERGENIC COATS

Not every Poodle mix is hypoallergenic. While Poodles and a few other dog breeds can be companions to those with pet allergies, there are many breeds that cannot. When looking at mixed breeds, you cannot know for certain that the dog will be hypoallergenic when he matures. You never know how the coat will develop or which parent's genes will be the most dominant. However, the chances are very good that the progeny of any dog mixed with Poodle parentage will have reduced shedding and a curlier, more dirt-resistant coat. And reduced vacuuming *is* part of what it's all about, isn't it?

undescended testicle would not be covered. Most breeders will offer a replacement puppy, but remember, if a defect shows up after you have had the pup for even a short while, it is unlikely that you will want to return him. He is already a member of your family. The very best breeders will negotiate with you and let you keep the pup, refunding all or a portion of your purchase price. For most people, it would be like trading in one of their children. Many defects don't show up until two years of age or later, and bear in mind that any breeder worth his salt will want to know about any health problem that develops even though the contract period may have elapsed. Breeders also appreciate follow-up by letter, phone or email and pictures of their puppies. Once again, it is a good idea to obtain a copy of the sales contract and puppy care information ahead of time so that you will be able to examine them and suggest changes that you want. There is way too much excitement when you pick up your new puppy to concentrate on these matters.

A fruitful breeding: three apricot pups at eight weeks.

Looking so soft and fluffy after
her first bath, 11-week-old Muffy
asks, "Are we ready to go home?"

CHOOSING THE PUPPY

The sex and color should be a lot less important than obtaining a puppy that is healthy and friendly. There are temperament tests that you can read about, and if you want to do some of these, be sure to ask the breeder's permission first. How a puppy was handled in its first six to eight weeks makes more difference in its adult life than its sex. Choose a dog for his manner, not his or her sex. Historically, males were more popular as people did not want to have the cost of spaying a female. Now just the opposite is true, and people are less concerned about the cost of spaying or neutering. Spaying a female, if you do not intend to breed, must be done early, before her first heat. Otherwise, the incidence of breast cancer in unspayed females who are not bred is very high. Spaying may alter your female dog's personality but not much else. Obesity has more to do with overfeeding and under-exercising than being spayed.

Neutering, or castration, also can alter a male dog's personality, largely because males are reproductive throughout the year. Yes, there is much publicity about dog overpopulation and the daunting reality of animals being put to death at shelters. But what responsible Cockapoo owner is going to let his male dog run loose around a neighborhood to inseminate all those females that have not been spayed? All vets will push you to have your puppy altered. There is no good reason to neuter a male if he is not running loose (except for the veterinarian's bank account). Vets will cite testicular cancer, which frightens human males (as well it should), but it is very rare in dogs. Besides, you can check the male dog's testicles for lumps along the way. If you are in a situation where your male dog is escaping your yard and running loose, you can opt for a vasectomy. It is fully as effective in preventing unwanted pregnancies but is not nearly as invasive. And a

HOW THEY'RE BRED

Few of the designer dogs are mixed hybrid to hybrid. Labradoodles, which have recently been recognized as a breed in Australia and are slowly being recognized as such in other parts of the world, are one of the few that go back up to 15 generations. Dogs are recognized as a breed if there are at least three generations of hybrid-to-hybrid breedings, producing standardized offspring with similar sizes and characteristics.

Most designer dogs are created by pairing pure-bred dogs together to achieve *hoped-for* results. The offspring will surely inherit some qualities from each parent. One won't know for certain without raising the dog and experiencing his temperament or viewing him as an adult.

vasectomy will not alter the personality of the dog. The biggest thing people fear about an unneutered male is that he will mount objects or people all the time. This behavior, common to both males and females, is easily discouraged right at the start.

Another big reason that this author encourages male Cockapoo owners to leave their boys whole is that there is a great shortage of stud dogs. If your male turns out to be a fine specimen of a Cockapoo, he may be in great demand as a stud. This will be an opportunity for you to obtain one of his progeny or collect stud fees or both. You love your dog so much and believe that he is so special (and he probably is) that you now want one of his pups. (Of course it goes without saying that you will have all of the proper and recommended genetic tests done before offering him as a stud.)

Neutering is the one action that is irreversible. The author's opinions do not necessarily apply in the world

of plentiful pure-bred breeds or mutts. But if the Cockapoo is to develop into a breed of its own, a choice of good stud dogs is essential to add to the genetic pool. Proof of the "Poo-ding," so to speak, is the number of Cockapoo breeders who turn to Poodle studs for the second generation because they cannot find suitable Cockapoo studs.

Males may have a more pronounced adolescence because of high testosterone levels that soon level off. It may be marked by an increase in mounting behavior and interest in mating. Mounting behavior is easily trained out but you do not want to do that if you anticipate using him as a stud. Instead, teach him to mount his "humping pillow" in private.

Only a small percentage of males go on to develop marking behavior in the house, especially when left alone, and they are saying "piss on you for leaving me." The few drops they do emit can be easily cleaned with a urine neutralizer and cleaning solution available from the pet-supply store. Other solutions are to crate the dog when you leave, use a "doggie diaper" (belly band with a sanitary pad inside) or restrict him to the kitchen or utility room. Even the best trained of housebroken females will urinate on the carpet occasionally (to say "piss on you"), leaving a big stain on the carpet that soaks down through the pad to the sub-flooring and is very difficult to get out.

Ask any breeder and he will tell you that the males are even sweeter than the females and are ever more loyal and devoted. It is said that females can be more easily disturbed by changes in the family and subject to mood swings. Females are just a little more tractable than males. Males and alpha females need a strong leader. In this case being a "control freak" is a good thing. If you are a person without much authority about you, purchase an easygoing, non-alpha female.

The Noah's Ark Option

If you're considering a pair of Cockapoos—and why not—there are some questions to answer. Should you buy two puppies from the same litter? The literature advises against this as the puppies may bond to each other and not to the owner. Some experts recommend acquiring a second dog at least three months later. The author, who would not sell two pups out of the same litter to one family, came upon one case of a bonding problem in all her years of breeding. Another breeder had sold a couple two males and found that they were bonding to each other instead of to the couple. In desperation they came to me because the breeder would not take a puppy back. Of course, I took the "extra" puppy and found him a good home.

On adding a new puppy when you have an older dog, select a puppy of the opposite sex. The next best option is to have two males and the worst choice is to have two females. With males, one will establish dominance in short order and they seldom fight. If they do, it is not usually vicious and just a matter of the alpha dog's putting the puppy in his place. The matter is settled. Two females, if they do not get along well and never establish dominance (or you may have two alpha females), will fight viciously and continuously and never settle anything. If you have more than two females, you have a pack with the nasty possibility of two or three ganging up on one. This can result in constant battles, severe injuries and even death.

The author with two lovely Cockapoo puppies, ready to board the Ark.

DOGFIGHTS

Keeping multiple Cockapoos, or any dogs, can result in dogfights, especially if you own more than one alpha female. From the author's experience, the best way to stop a dogfight is with a hose. For some reason, most serious fights seem to occur outdoors. Inside, if the dogs are of equal size and strength, it may be best to leave them alone for a bit. Stepping in and trying to disentangle the dogs is dangerous, but sometimes it has to be done, especially if there is a disparity in size or strength. If you are alone and no hose is handy, grab each dog high on the scruff of the neck and physically pull them apart and hold them that way until they calm down. (Needless to say, while letting them know, in no uncertain terms, that fighting is not permitted.) If there is more than one person, some people advise that each person should pull a dog by the tail. This maneuver is not comfortable for the dog and in the frenzy, she may turn around and bite you. Lifting by the scruff of neck is a lot safer. Moral of the story: always keep a hose handy with the water turned on.

It's raining "Poo" pups.

Your New *Cockapoo* Puppy

Preparations need to be made before you actually collect your new puppy. Much of this is similar to preparing for the arrival of a new human baby. There is the layette, sometimes even "new puppy showers" and preparation of a special place within your home. It is an opportunity for every member of the household to participate, learn and grow. Both parents and children should be involved as much as possible. As age permits, children can be assigned to read about feeding, care, crate training, etc. They can start a "baby book," which will become a record of the pup's lineage, shots, first experiences and so forth. New-puppy books are sold in major pet-supply centers, or children can be creative and make their own. Children and dogs form a natural bond, and the dogs of childhood are never forgotten. In many, many cases, it is the children's insistence that prompts the parents to buy a puppy in the first place. The "I'll walk him every day" or "I'll feed him" promises may soon be forgotten. Ultimately, the parents are responsible for care and feeding or seeing that it is done. Adding a puppy to your household is a great joy and provides a wonderful range of lessons in "responsible parenting" to your children.

A special place in your home that is safe and warm needs to be set aside for the pup. Go shopping for a layette. Perhaps organizing a "new puppy" party would be a fun theme for your children.

let's throw a "new puppy" shower!

At the top of your list of things to buy will be a crate. There is a variety of designs, from fiberglass to wire, in an array of colors. Most prefer fiberglass because they come closest to representing the den, a place to hide and be safe. Crates can be obtained in pet stores or pet-supply centers. The first crate needs to be just big enough so that the pup will be able to stand up and turn around. Although most books recommend buying a crate that is large enough to accommodate the size of the grown dog, this author feels that it is better to start off with a small one and graduate to a larger one as the pup grows. You will need toys and food, sturdy food and water bowls, a 6-foot nylon lead and a buckle collar. Cockapoos do not need choke chains, and don't waste money on harnesses or retractable leashes as the latter only teach the dog to pull.

Choosing a veterinarian is very important, and probably the best way to do this is to use a vet recommended by your friends or acquaintances who own dogs. Make an appointment with the vet before you bring your puppy home. The

Here's a multi-colored Cockapoo puppy, all dressed up for winter.

vet will give the pup a physical exam and set a schedule for the series of immunizations that will be needed. The breeder will have had the puppies inoculated once before releasing them.

A healthy, happy Cockapoo puppy, settling into his new home.

THE BEST START IN LIFE
Ideally, if you chose a good breeder, your puppy will have been given the finest possible start in life:
• Born of fine tempered, healthy parents, who have been certified free of inherited eye disease, hip and elbow dysplasia and patellar luxation.
• Wormed and fully immunized for his age with state-of-the-art vaccine.
• Kept in the home or in a nursery, warm, clean and free of pests.
• Fed the highest quality diet.
• Provided with veterinary supervision.
• Had dewclaws removed for safety.
• Given plenty of loving attention and provided with training experiences and socialization that coincide with his developmental stages.

Puppies love stringy things. Keep ribbon away from your pup's mouth and paws.

PUPPY SAFETY AROUND THE HOUSE

Raising a puppy is much like raising a toddler. Puppy-proof your home and yard. Puppies do not discriminate between chewable objects. They will sink their teeth into anything, so look for dangers such as electrical cords, telephone cords, plants and household cleaning products. Many plants, both indoors and out, are poisonous, so make sure your puppy cannot ingest them.

Puppies seem to have a natural affinity for electrical and telephone cords. The best thing to do is to wipe them all down with a product designed to deter chewing (available in pet stores). It tastes terrible and can also be sprayed on stool if the pup tends to eat it (natural for the dog but disgusting to us).

Fit your pup with a buckle collar. Collars can be a hazard if they are put on too loosely and the pup gets his jaw caught in it, sometimes even his front leg. The collar should be snug enough so that you can only slip two fingers under it and should be checked at frequent intervals as the pup grows.

Several human foods can be lethal when ingested by a dog: it would take only 2 ounces of baker's chocolate to kill a 20-pound dog. Don't keep this a secret: be sure all members of your household know not to use a chocolate bar as a training treat. The smaller the dog, the less it would take. The same goes for caffeine as in regular coffee or espresso. Onions and their relatives, garlic and chives, can also be toxic, causing anemia and stomach problems. Nuts and alcohol can also be lethal. Seeing a dog drunk and staggering from drinking beer is not funny and may result in the dog's death. Raisins and grapes have been responsible for several deaths in small dogs. One cannot be too careful in handling both prescription and over-the-counter drugs. Many tablets are sugar-coated and very attractive to a dog.

Antifreeze leaked from a car is probably one of the leading killers of dogs and cats.

It has a natural sweet aroma that attracts them. Cleaning products, disinfectants, pesticides and rodent killers are toxic if ingested and so are many aerosol sprays and other deodorizers when inhaled. (Pet birds and cats are particularly sensitive to inhaled toxins.) Many dogs like to nibble on grass and that can become problematic if the lawn has been sprayed with chemicals.

Following is a list of common toxic indoor and outdoor plants: azalea, bird of paradise, bulbs (hyacinth, narcissus family), calla lily, castor bean, chinaberry tree, daphne, dieffenbachia, elephant's ear, hydrangea, jasmine, jimsonweed, larkspur (delphinium), laurel, lily of the valley, mescal bean, mushrooms, nightshades, philodendron, poinsettia, tobacco, yellow jasmine and yews.

For first-aid sake, it is wise, when one has small children or pets, to keep on hand 3% peroxide solution or syrup of Ipecac (not tincture) to induce vomiting.

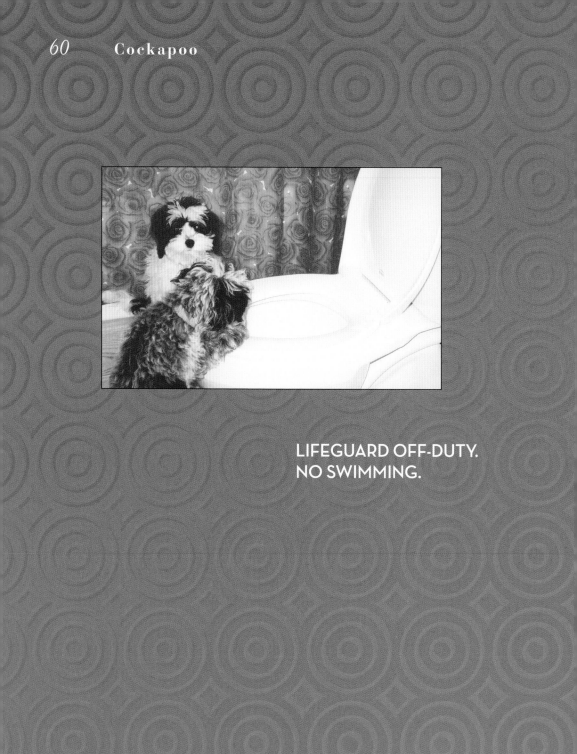

LIFEGUARD OFF-DUTY.
NO SWIMMING.

BRINGING PUPPY HOME

Remember that the puppy is going to have to make some very big adjustments. He may never have been in a car before so should ride in his crate where he will remain safe and comfortable. He may also get carsick so be prepared with some old towels.

The first days can be very trying for both the puppy and the new owner, similar to bringing an infant home. The main challenges for the new family are crate training and housebreaking, and for the puppy, learning to sleep by himself without the warmth and comfort of his littermates and finding out what his place is in the "pecking order" of your household. Your pup is ready to learn at 4 weeks, but teaching and learning require frequent and consistent repetitions of the same commands, anywhere from 100–200 times before he "gets it."

For quiet breaks and sleeping, the crate is your most valuable tool. A stuffed animal, soft bedding (or a towel) and a chew toy or two are all the puppy needs to settle down when "crate time" falls. Those sterilized hollow bones, stuffed with peanut butter, will entertain for hours. You can also feed the pup in his crate, but never leave food or water inside it.

Remember that the pup is used to sleeping squashed in with his littermates. They all piled on top of each other. Some people bring a blanket or towel from the breeder's home to aid in the transition. It also may be helpful for the bonding process for you to put an unwashed piece of your clothing in the bed, such as a T-shirt, so that he gets to know your scent.

The crate is his den and is a natural place of safety and protection. The pup will instinctively know not to soil his bed and will only do so if ill or left in too long. This is the reason for a small crate. Otherwise, if the crate is too big, he may use one end for a potty station and the other for a sleeping area. Pups need a lot of sleep and if you have children, see that the pup does not get overtired and teach the kids to respect the pup's privacy when he is in his crate.

A pup has three ways to communicate his needs: whining, crying and screaming. The first behavior is okay but crying and especially screaming are to be eliminated. For this reason, never remove the pup from his crate while he is crying or screaming. This just rewards the behavior and encourages more of the same. He must be quiet for 30 seconds before opening the door. Talking to him soothingly will usually work to quiet him. Part of the "talk" can be counting out the 30 seconds of time.

The first week or so, he may have to be taken out to eliminate once or twice during the night. Don't jump out of bed on the first peep; wait to see if he is serious. Sometimes just saying a few words will reassure him, and you will not have to get up. The most difficult thing for you will be to not give in and allow him to sleep in your bed. Break training, even once, and it is very difficult to get back on track. So do yourself and him a favor and insist he sleep in his crate with the door closed. Most owners find that placing the crate next to their bed gives the puppy enough security and company. As long as the pup can smell and hear you, he'll fall fast asleep in no time.

Not a peep out of this tiny Poo.

FEEDING

If your puppy is not already on a premium dog food from the breeder, switch him slowly to the new food over a period of ten days. To do otherwise may result in diarrhea. Feed only a dry premium dog food made especially for puppies. For tiny puppies, get the "small bite" variety made by many manufacturers. Premium dog food is only sold at pet stores or vets' offices. Most brands found in grocery stores use inferior-quality ingredients. Do you want your dog getting his protein from chicken feathers and beaks or from backs and giblets? Premium dog foods may seem more expensive but the dog eats a lot less to get the nutrition he needs and digests it better with less waste. This results in small, hard stools which massage the anal glands on the way out. The author feels that most of the problems seen with anal glands today are due to the soft stools passed by our dogs. There must be a connection between years of feeding a premium brand and never having a problem with

A DESIGNER DIET FOR ALL DOGS

Few dogs thrive on corn-based diets. You will rarely see a dog choose an ear of corn over a piece of meat. Dogs are omnivorous but require a good majority of their food to be meat-based. A quality dog food should contain meat as the main ingredient, and the remaining ingredients should include vegetables, brewer's yeast/rice, vitamins and omega fatty acids. Preservatives are not only a sign that rancid ingredients were used in the manufacturing of the food but can also be damaging, over time, to your dog's internal organs.

Veterinarians and breeders will normally steer their clients either to the brand they sell or have been using with their own dogs. Ask them why that particular food is one they recommend. What are the key nutrients? Why will this particular food give the dog a glowing coat and spring in his step?

The easiest means of choosing a food is to read the label. The first three ingredients are those that comprise the majority of the food. You should see actual meat within the first three ingredients, meaning beef, chicken, lamb, fish or venison, not meal or corn or rice hulls. Actual meat. If you have a dog with meat allergies, try a fish- or venison-based diet.

Meat, it's what's for dinner!

A premium diet for a premium designer puppy!

This is another area in which you need to stay disciplined. Once you get a dog used to canned food, it will be very difficult to go back to dry. And dogs need to chew! Leaving food down all the time (called "free feeding") is not recommended because studies have shown that puppies fed this way consume 20% more than they need. Not only does this lead to obesity but also to bone defects later in life. It is better to have your pup a little underweight.

Make no fuss about eating. It is a natural and neutral behavior and should not be encouraged or discouraged. The "clean plate club" does not apply to dogs. Except in rare cases of illness, the dog will eat exactly what he needs. Both pups and adult dogs will occasionally skip a meal. Keep fresh water available at all times, except in the crate. You should limit water intake in the evening until the puppy is fully housebroken.

Not feeding table scraps is the best policy. As studies have shown, even the most innocent-sounding people food can be

anal glands in any of my dogs.

Feed large pups twice a day and smaller ones three times a day at first. Offer dry food, as much as they will eat in 15 minutes, and then pick up the food until the next mealtime. Do not moisten or add canned food.

toxic, even lethal, to dogs. Avoid feeding table scraps. If you must, they should not comprise more than 10% of the dog's total intake. This 10% would include commercial dog treats that have little or no nutritional value. Only give a treat when the dog earns it for doing something. Do not offer your dog any real bones except the sterilized beef knuckle bones, as other kinds may splinter and perforate the gastrointestinal tract.

Your premium food is a perfectly balanced formula and not meant to be supplemented with anything else. Let us cast out old beliefs about growing puppies needing extra vitamins, cottage cheese, milk or eggs. They not only are unnecessary but may cause a host of skeletal and cartilage defects. They may also decrease phosphorus, iron, zinc and copper absorption and cause crusty and scaly skin. Also limit rawhides, pigs' ears and such to occasional treats. Hooves are great because they take so long to eat, giving good chewing exercise without adding much to the diet.

People food is for the birds—limit treats and table scraps from puppyhood.

HOUSE-TRAINING

Here, as in all training, structure, consistency, repetition and positive reinforcement are of paramount importance to the speed of your success. There are books on the market that tell you about training your dog in seven days and such. Don't believe it! You are the one who is trained. Four months of age is about the best you can hope for a pup to become consistent in his toilet habits.

The routine is fairly simple, starting with day one. Carry the pup outside or to his designated potty area as soon as he awakens, after meals and every hour while awake. Soon you will learn to read the "signals" indicating he needs to go. Put him down (teacup toys can be taught to use a litter pan), and when he squats to urinate, use a command such as "Go tinkle" or "Go potty" and praise him lavishly when he does. See how soon he learns to look up at you for his praise when he squats. A tiny food treat may also be used some of the time. Do the same for his bowel movement and before you know it, you will have a dog that goes on command. It is most important that you go out with him each time so you are there to praise him. Urinary continence will most likely come first, as that is done so frequently. Pups do not have a bowel movement each time you take them out, so that takes longer to learn. You will soon learn to predict times of bowel movement if you are feeding him as instructed. (Another negative aspect of free feeding is the difficulty of predicting bowel movements.) If training to the yard, it's a good idea not to play with him out there at first so that he learns its primary purpose.

When you cannot keep an eye on the puppy, put him in his crate with something to entertain him. Accidents happen, and there is no value in scolding a puppy for an accident after the fact. If you catch him in the act, you may yell "No" and grab him up quickly. If you are quick enough, you may stop him in midstream and he will continue outside and get his praise. Never spank him or rub his nose in his "accident." This

Potty On Command

Just as you teach commands for many desired behaviors, it's also very convenient to have your dog potty on command. This will save many frustrating outings, waiting in bad weather or anxious that you'll be late for work because Junior is taking his sweet time, sniffing, playing and avoiding the reason he was brought to his relief area.

Begin by going outside with your pup first thing in the morning. At this time of day, it's a sure thing that he *must* go immediately. Say the *potty* word (such as "Go," "Hurry," "Business" or "Potty") over and over until he goes. The moment he goes, praise him. Give him a treat when he is finished.

Every time you take your pup to his relief area, say the word over and over until he relieves himself. Repeat the rewarding words and treats as before. Within a week, Junior will potty on command.

Teaching the Cockapoo his basic lessons can take a couple of months—no need to put your puppy on the "fast track."

is not only disgusting but also useless and harmful. It makes the dog fear and distrust his master and teaches the dog to potty where you cannot see him. For accidents, clean up out of the pup's view. First soak up urine with an old towel, then soak the area with a urine odor neutralizer and sop that up. There should be no residual odor to draw the pup back to that spot.

In the case of small Cockapoos or during inclement weather, you may wish to begin training to newspapers or you can buy "wee-wee" pads at the pet store, which are impregnated with a scent to attract the pup to them. The pads are much preferred to newspaper as they keep the pup clean and are much more absorbent. The pads can be placed in a small enclosed area such as the utility room or shower stall.

And finally, a reminder: allow the puppy in only a small space in your home until he is completely trustworthy in the house. Once he tastes freedom and gets to explore the whole house, it is extremely difficult to go back. In all my years of dealing with people and their new puppies, this is the most common single mistake that is made: too much freedom, too soon!

CRATE FACTS

In the wild, canines prefer to sleep and raise their young in dens, which are small, enclosed areas where the dogs feel safely surrounded on all sides and able to sense an intruder approaching. At very early ages, puppies learn to relieve themselves outside the den, as that is where they smell the deposits of other dogs, which attracts them to that location.

Using a crate for your pup during house-training recreates this instinctual behavior, giving your pup the security he desires and teaching him to contain himself when you cannot be there to take him to his relief area. As he cannot move around much, he won't need to relieve himself as often. Using the crate will help you gain control of his scheduling as well as help you teach Junior to potty on command, for you will know that he will definitely have to relieve himself the moment you let him out of his crate.

Designer dog, having a ball.

IMMUNIZATIONS AND WORMING

Within a week of arriving to his new home, the sooner the better, your pup needs to be taken to the vet for a physical exam and schedule for further immunizations and worming. If a congenital anomaly is found, it's best to return the pup immediately before complete bonding has occurred and it is too late and too painful. Immunizations cover a variety of canine diseases such as distemper, parvovirus, hepatitis, coronavirus and leptospirosis. Be sure that the vet does not give a vaccine with leptospirosis to a pup under 10 lbs as it can have severe side effects. Other immunizations such as *Giardia*, Lyme disease and infectious traechobronchitis should be considered depending on your lifestyle. Rabies vaccination is mandatory in every state.

Just as distemper used to be the big killer of puppies, today parvovirus is the most feared by breeders. It is a highly contagious disease that causes diarrhea and vomiting and is often fatal. Be sure to ask your vet about its prevalence in your area and for guidance on safe puppy socialization.

The reason that a puppy needs a series of shots is because antibodies in the mother's milk may interfere with the vaccine's effectiveness. The antibodies wane between 8 and 16 weeks, but there is no way of telling when that will occur in any particular pup. There is likely to be a "window of time" when the antibody level drops and the pup gets his next shot. The pup is then susceptible and, if exposed to parvovirus, may get the disease. The disease is somewhat breed-specific, and the Cockapoo is not as vulnerable as a lot of other breeds. Parvovirus is passed in the infected stools and urine of infected dogs and is also airborne, is very hardy and can last in the environment for a year or two. The virus can even be carried into your home on your shoes.

Sadly, you cannot keep your puppy in a "sterile bubble" as he also has socialization needs that must be met during this time frame. It is a balancing act that you must maneuver using your vet's advice. Avoid bringing the Cockapoo puppy to places where dogs of unknown health may visit, such as the pet supermarket and dog parks, until his immunizations are complete. Your puppy may have contact with adult dogs that you know are fully immunized. As cute as it is to see two puppies playing together, other puppies are at the most risk of harboring the infection. After your pup's last shot, it is safe (and recommended) to take your pup to puppy kindergarten classes.

Look mom, no worms!

Socialization

Puppy kindergarten classes are the best investment you will ever make in your puppy, your family and yourself, even if you think you already know how to train a dog. Besides being a lot of fun, these classes will help you see how mellow and trainable your Cockapoo is compared to most other dogs in the class. Please do not gloat because you had the good sense to get a Cockapoo! A well-trained dog will have a healthy ego and feel secure and loved. Your pup needs to meet a wide variety of people and other dogs and be taken to a variety of places: rides in the car, to the bank, inside stores that allow dogs, etc. You and he will get a million dollars' worth of free socialization. This will make for an outgoing, friendly dog. If you don't have your own kids, make an effort to expose your dog to children so he will always consider them his friends.

BATHING AND GROOMING

Training for grooming starts as soon as your puppy comes home. During lap times, get him used to being handled all over, looking in his ears and mouth and touching the sensitive areas. Make it gentle and fun. Begin to comb gently while talking or singing to him and praise lavishly for any quiet, accepting behavior. Later, add the noise of an electric clipper. Soon introduce a doggie toothbrush and paste. And still later, train him to stand on a table to be groomed.

Never allow the puppy to growl or bite for any reason. Grooming sessions are the most likely times that your dog will challenge your authority. Any aggressive behavior calls for immediate, swift and very stern intervention. He needs to know that you are the "alpha dog" in his pack and that when you say "groom time" there's no discussion. Then continue gentle grooming, praising all the while for any signs of cooperation.

Always comb thoroughly before bathing to assure there are no mats. Bathe your puppy only when necessary as frequent bathing can result in drying out the skin. Once every two weeks is probably sufficient. Use a puppy "no more tears" shampoo. Wash in lukewarm water, avoid getting shampoo in the eyes or ears, rinse well and towel dry, all the while speaking softly and reassuringly to the puppy. You can blow dry on low, but get him used to the noise first. Begin with the dryer at some distance and give him a couple of treats, then gradually move it toward him. Start by drying his rear end (they hate it in their faces) and gradually creep up the body, keeping up a line of "good boy" chatter. Help from another person is nice, at least for the first few times.

Comb your pup daily or at least twice a week, using a metal comb that has teeth long enough to reach down to the skin. Get him used to having his ears inspected and cleaned and your fingers

Do you want to play?

Toys and Treats

Puppies love soft squeak toys, rawhide bones, sterilized hollow bones in which you can slip a piece of meat or peanut butter, cows' hooves, tug-of-war toys, balls and pigs' ears. Pigs' ears, rawhides and other such easily eaten items are not recommended as they add too much protein to the diet and can be dangerous if pieces are swallowed. There are differences of opinion about playing tug of war. Some authorities feel that it will make the dog aggressive. General guidance is to stand up so you are in the dominant position and can control the game. Occasionally, the pup may lose a baby tooth that was ready to come out anyway. Gentle play and letting the dog win sometimes is okay.

As a training reward, small bites of beef jerky or liver treats are good. The dog feels just as rewarded by a small piece as he does by the entire stick. The smaller the dog, the smaller the treat!

in his mouth in preparation for brushing teeth later. Make yourself and the pup comfortable when you do this, perhaps seated in your favorite chair with the pup on your lap. Use a table and chair to prepare for a groomer, should you decide to use one later. Good preventive cleaning of the ears is extremely important. Be sure to clean inside the ears with a cotton ball and pull the excess hair out of the ears with a tweezer. (Ask your breeder or groomer to show you how to do this and how to cut the toenails.) If you smell an unpleasant odor, if you see dark wax or if the pup shakes his head a lot, a vet check is in order.

It is a good idea to take the dog to a groomer after he has finished his shots, even if you do not intend to use one regularly, so he gets used to someone else handling him. Choose a groomer by recommendation only and use one who keeps the dog for only a few hours, not all day. If you decide to have your Cockapoo clipped, be very specific about what

"Come," they told me.

The "Come" Command

Next to house-training, this is the most important command that your dog will ever learn and obeying it may someday save his life. The trick is simple: Always reward the come command in some way. Start out in a small space with "Adam, come." Praise lavishly for coming and give a treat some of the time. Remember Skinner in Psychology 101, in which the rats learned best by a schedule of variable and random reinforcement? Never call the pup to you to scold him, put him in his crate, groom him or anything else that could be construed as a mildly unpleasant activity. When you need him to do something, go and get him. Do these things consistently and you should have a dog that comes, no matter what he is doing. The author even had a dog obey the come command in the midst of chasing a rabbit!

Don't spoil your Cockapoo by fussing too much over his coat. The natural look is in!

you want and present the groomer with written instructions, along with a phone number where you can be reached. Unless you tell a groomer to scissor the coat to a specific length, he will usually take the path of least resistance and shave with a guard on the clippers. The result is a shaved dog—very unattractive.

The most attractive Cockapoos are those left in their natural state with long hair. Leave a full face and goatee, shaving only the top of the nose and slightly under the eyes to make the eyes visible and mustache and goatee prominent. Scissor the topknot just enough to keep hair out of eyes. Ears should be left long and only trimmed on the ends. Leave the tail full and natural. Shaving around the belly, genitals and rectum helps to keep these areas clean and free of knots. The under-pads of the feet may also be shaved, but not the top as in the Poodle.

SPOILED POOS

To get your pup used to staying alone, leave him in his crate and go out for varying periods of time, whether you need to or not. Do not make a big fuss over him when leaving or returning. Leave a radio or TV on if you wish. Owners, especially of small, cute, fuzzy, appealing dogs like Cockapoos, tend to forget they are dogs and use their dogs to satisfy their need to nurture something, sometimes to an excessive degree. This may result in the dog becoming a spoiled, overfed, finicky and overly anxious dog with few, if any, boundaries. He will not be welcome in people's homes because he neurotically pesters everyone for attention, marks in the house, mounts people's legs and so forth. Owners create a situation where they feel they cannot go anywhere without their precious pooch, thus limiting their lives since dogs cannot go everywhere. You all know people like this, and it is your choice about whether you want to become one of them, or show real love for your dog by training him and teaching him manners.

Here's a half dozen good and colorful reasons to breed your Cockapoo!

Attention Designer Dog Breeders..

Most people start to think

about breeding for one of the following reasons: "get their money back," "an experience for the children," the myth that "having one litter will settle your bitch down," and lastly to "work toward making the Cockapoo into a breed." The last reason is the only valid one.

Keep in mind that your pet can die in the process of giving birth. That would be some "experience for the children"! She can also frighten them by chewing the cord too close and ripping the puppy's abdomen open or cannibalizing the pups. Most children are upset by all the blood and guts of deliveries. And what child wants to get up at 1 A.M.? There are plenty of good videos available to show children the miracle of birth.

You may indeed spend more on vet care, feeding and housing than you get for the pups. An unexpected Caesarian section or a puppy in intensive care may make a break-even litter a big liability. If you paid a high price for your dog, you probably acquired her from a very experienced breeder who has spent years developing a reputation and a business. You cannot begin to compete with this type of breeder, and even with the designer-dog craze, it is unlikely that you will be able to command such high prices.

Your female must be either spayed before her first heat (usually about six months old) or reserved for breeding. An unspayed female

Breeding Resources

When the author is asked to mentor a new breeder, the first thing I do is have them read a book on labor and delivery. There are several on the market but a personal favorite is *Successful Dog Breeding* by Chris Walkowicz and Bonnie Wilcox, DVM. It covers all of the bases with lots of good humor while still addressing the tragedies that can and do occur. Even if you are breeding only one dog, you need to develop a good basis and familiarity with the standard, Code of Ethics and above all genetics. You will be expected to know a great deal not only about breeding and whelping but also about raising puppies. Another excellent resource is *Whelping and Raising Puppies* by Muriel P. Lee, a standard that has been in print for many years.

who is never bred has a much greater risk of breast cancer, as well as uterine and ovarian cancer and uterine infections, than the one spayed at six months. The longer you wait to spay, the greater the risk. So the decision has to be made early. The most popular myth or old wives' tale is that letting your dog have one litter will "settle her down." Age, maturity and especially training settle her down, not delivering and nursing a litter of puppies.

Even though you may think you will be able to place all the puppies in good homes, all the promises of "I want a dog just like yours" have a magical way of evaporating. One can even discuss the probability that your pups would not sell, though this is hardly likely with the high demand for Cockapoos. Some authorities feel that the "backyard breeder" or hobby breeding contribute to the pet overpopulation by removing clients from the pool of people who would otherwise adopt from the local shelters and humane societies. Every year in the US alone over 20 million animals wind up in shelters and over half of them are euthanized.

You may think your Cockapoo has an outstanding personality and is a fine example of the "breed," but best leave that to an unbiased opinion. You will need several things to consider breeding: a stud that complements your female and is not related, a mentor and a thirst for knowledge so that you read and learn all you can to be the best breeder possible.

As to raising puppies, you must be prepared for the amount of work involved. After the first two or three weeks, during which the mother takes care of all of the pups' needs, puppies become little "poop factories." And they step in it, get it stuck on their rear ends and every place else. So picking up and cleaning is a constant labor. We know the kids promised to help—but somehow they are not around or become too busy—so it's up to you!

Almost everything one reads about obtaining a puppy of any breed tells the reader to go to an expert. This is certainly wise counsel but even those "experts" were novices at one time. So the novice has to begin somewhere and hopefully it is with good mentors. Currently there are not enough breeders to meet the demand for Cockapoos, so newcomers with honorable intentions are welcome. Always remember that there is a lot more to be gained by cooperating than by competing. The only kind of competition between breeders that would be good for the Cockapoo would be trying to "out excel" each other.

Both home and kennel breeders have their merits. The breeder who owns a kennel can have several different lines going, usually has a lot of expertise on genetics and whelping and can keep his own studs. The main problem with some kennel breeders is the potential lack of human exposure for pups and dogs. But the good ones see to it that all dogs and pups are handled and played with, and they usually bring their females inside to

Shower your puppies with
love and affection.

deliver or have a special nursery. The home breeder on the other hand will be limited in the number of dogs and usually does not keep his own studs. Usually puppies are showered with love, kept exceptionally clean and warm and have the experience of home, children, yard and grass. There are all shades and varieties of kennel owners as there are home breeders.

Some other things to think about: the mother cannot be left alone during labor or delivery, and only briefly for several days thereafter. Do you work? How are you going to arrange to be home when labor starts? If you can't provide the time, you will either have dead pups or poor ones, perhaps dirty and/or sickly—hardly a buyer's delight!

Okay, you have decided, and your goal is "breed" improvement. Here are some of the things you need to know before you start.

Study and make Cockapoos your passion. Learn at least the basics of genetics and all you can about rearing and training

The Code

Another very important thing to consider is your own temperament and moral value. Are you the type who can just take the money and have no concern about what kind of a life this puppy is going to have? Or will you carefully screen potential buyers? Would you take back a grown dog that you bred if the owners are no longer able to care for him? Is one of your "grand-pups" chained in a yard, left with little or no attention and at the mercy of the elements and predators? Are you prepared to live by the Cockapoo Club of America's Breeder Code of Ethics?

puppies. And like any professional, you must keep up on the latest developments! Many university veterinary schools publish their own newsletters with the latest scientific evidence on a variety of canine matters. One of the author's favorites is Cornell University's *DogWatch* magazine. There is a ton of information on the Internet; not all of it is reliable, though much of it is excellent with good references.

Meanwhile, all we have to go on is what a particular dog looks like (what we call the phenotype) and the genetic testing that has gone before. All depends on which genes are dominant in each dog. This can be determined to some degree by both looking back at the progenitors and looking forward at the progeny. There is also another big factor in there and that is environment: how pups are raised, the type of food, parasites, etc. No matter how good the genetic makeup, a

Infant asleep . . .

BASIC GENETIC TERMS

One cannot begin a discussion about breeding without knowing some very basic genetic terms. Phenotype is what you can see, the composite Cockapoo, the "looks and feel" of a show dog or one most closely resembling the standard. Genotype is the dog's genetic makeup, what you don't

dog will not grow to his full genetic potential if he is full of parasites and fed a poor diet.

An example about determining genotype is my little "Hercules." He came from a line of small Cockapoos but not teacups, and he turned out to be a teacup toy. I was able to determine, after breeding him with many different females, that he had a gene or genes for the teacup size. He always produced at least one teacup toy in a litter, even when bred to females weighing 15 pounds. I also learned more about his color,

called pseudo-phantom (pseudo-phantom is a dog that is born a silver brindle that turns phantom at about a year of age). So he consistently produced silver brindle pups, true phantom pups, pseudo-phantoms and rarely a cream like his father "Lamb Chop," no matter the coloring of the female.

And so, wisdom would dictate that you breed "the best to the best." But you cannot base all your decisions

see. Dogs have 39 chromosomes and 50–100,000 genes. The process to map the dog's genes and DNA is underway at the Baker Institute at Cornell University's Veterinary School. When this is done and the genetic map is available at reasonable cost, it will revolutionize the dog world.

Ready for play!

Ready, world, for a confident little Cockapoo! Here's Teegan at eight weeks of age.

like a Cocker, one like a Poodle and two will look like Cockapoos. The next expectation is that if you breed a Cockapoo-looking first generation to an unrelated Cockapoo-looking first generation, out of four second-generation pups, perhaps three out of four will look like Cockapoos and so on down the lines. The experience of breeders seems to hold pretty true to that theory. First-generation dogs are producing occasional dogs that shed and some that look like neither Poodle, Cocker nor Cockapoo. It would drive a breeder mad! By continuous outcrossing (not breeding related pairs), we have attempted to avoid the genetic faults promoted by inbreeding or line-breeding. Outcrossing has worked with the Parson Russell Terrier and those breeders wound up with a dog that looks like a Parson Russell and has been recognized by the AKC as a breed. The Parson Russell Terrier is one of the breeds least affected by genetic problems.

on phenotype. A breeder needs to know about the dogs' genotype regarding physical traits, temperament and health.

In breeding first-generation Cockapoos, it is expected that out of four pups, one will look

BREEDING OPTIONS

In the world of designer dogs there are two options when it comes to breeding: crossbreeding, which means pairing the parental breeds, or breeding two Cockapoos together the way pure-bred dog breeders do. There are three types of breeding used in the pure-bred dog fancy: inbreeding, line-breeding and outcrossing. Inbreeding is the mating of closely related pairs, mother/son, father/daughter and brother/sister. The advantage of doing this type of breeding is that you can achieve type quickly. Line-breeding is the breeding of related pairs, but not as close as inbreeding: half brother/half sister, first cousins, etc. This also locks the type fairly rapidly, i.e., the dogs reproduce themselves. The third type of breeding, outcrossing, is the mating of unrelated members of the same breed, often utilized to bring in "new blood" or improve a particular feature.

Regarding breeding related dogs, this can also concentrate undesirable genes together.

Teegan, growing up, at ten weeks of age. Owner, Camano Island kennel.

There is a good reason that inbreeding human beings is not sanctioned in our society. Some authors claim that all the defects, both physical and mental, in today's pure-breds are the result of too much inbreeding. Or is it too much inbreeding by breeders who don't know what they are doing? Richard Beauchamp, a well-respected AKC and UKC judge, breeder and author of *Breeding Dogs for Dummies*, states that, "An experienced breeder knows that if the individuals in use are line-bred, the likelihood of their reproducing themselves is very high. However, if you use an individual from an outcross breeding or one whose pedigree is primarily the result of outcross breedings, chances of retaining any continuity become increasingly less likely. The chances of unknown or unanticipated characteristics—those things I call the X factors—appearing also increase." This author goes on to say, "In too many cases, survival of the breed has taken a back seat, if it has a seat at all, to marks of beauty. For some breeds, rigid selection for conformation has taken precedence over longevity. Genetic disorders run rampant and cause early death."

This author is reminded of what humans have done to various canine and feline breeds. The Collie is bred with such a narrow head that some detractors believe the dog does not have much room left for a brain. The Bulldog is bred for such wide chests that it can no longer mate nor give birth naturally and are not even allowed to raise its own puppies for fear it will crush them. The latter, in my opinion, is one of the worst travesties created by man. And why is the breed club supporting this and the AKC allowing these dogs to be shown? It is not what the original Bulldog was supposed to represent but a caricature of a dog that cannot breed or raise its young. I don't know how anyone can do this to an animal!

And so, a new breeder has the option of acquiring the original parental breeds or purchasing first- or second-generation Cockapoos for

+ +

Start Your Own Stud Book

This is a book (or computer program) in which all matters pertaining to pedigrees, genetic testing, matings, litters, etc., are recorded. Hopefully you are starting with AKC provable stock. If you have pure-bred Cockers and Poodles, and no papers are available, you can contact the AKC for a DNA testing kit. This will prove, with only a 1% error rate, that your stock is pure Poodle and Cocker. Remember that AKC registration papers have nothing to do with quality. They are merely records, databases of information put in by human beings. Human beings make mistakes and papers are only as good as the honesty of the person filling them out. The AKC (www.akc.org) has volumes of material that will be helpful to a new breeder, and you are encouraged to learn all you can. Also, the website for the Cockapoo Club of America (www.cockapooclub.com) has lots of helpful information, forms and instructions you can print.

Face it, there are mutts in the background of every pooch on the planet.

Salud!
Here's to healthy,
beautiful Cockapoos!

breeding. The latter is recommended because it is very difficult to find a good AKC breeder who has done all the genetic testing and is willing to sell you his dogs with the intent of creating a "mutt." Most good AKC breeders sell only with spay and neuter contracts. This means that they will not give you the papers until you submit proof of sterilization. And you need papers to prove

that your Cockapoo is really a Cockapoo and to register it with the NACR (www.cockapoos.com). Hopefully, this book and the work of the CCA will help to enlighten some AKC breeders and judges. The one exception to finding good specimens of the parental breeds is to find good Cockapoo breeders who also breed one or both of the parental breeds.

Don't write me off
as a mere write-off.

OTHER CONSIDERATIONS

Another must if you are going to become a breeder is to check out your local county ordinances regarding the number of dogs allowed, licensing requirements and fees and requirements for business licenses. Get acquainted with your local animal-control officer and local shelter, perhaps offering to do a "Cockapoo rescue" for any Cockapoos that wind up there. And of course establish a good relationship with your vet, choosing one who has lots of experience in dog reproduction. If you are in or near a large metropolis or a veterinary school, you can even acquire the services of canine reproduction specialists. Veterinary medicine has just about all the specialties that human medicine has, along with board certifications.

It is hardly ever advisable for a home breeder to keep his own stud. The howling and grieving when females are in estrus will drive you crazy, not to mention how frustrating it is for the poor stud. Either find a local Don Juan or give a stud to a very stable family as a pet with a lifetime stud contract. This latter arrangement works out nicely for all concerned but you must make sure, as sure as sure can be, that the family is not going to move. The contract should cover this possibility. And of course, you can always ship your female for breeding.

Even if no business license is required, you need to register your kennel as a business. Establish a kennel name, keep accounting records that will measure up to an IRS audit and report earnings. Even if you are only breeding one dog, you should report the single litter. Of course, all dog-related expenses are balanced against income. Expenses include cost of stock, vet fees, food and supplies, laundry and a share of utilities and upkeep of that portion of the home and yard reserved for the dogs. Even mileage to and from the vet, other breeders and the pet-supply store is included.

The author was a home breeder and the business, All American Cockapoos, was audited by the IRS. After everything was proven to be on the up and up, the agent took me out for coffee. In his 25 years with the IRS, he had never seen a dog breeder show a profit and wanted to know why. The only thing I could guess was that AKC breeders had a lot more expenses in registration fees and travel to and from shows. This is how a breeder can honestly say, "I never make any money on my dogs." This statement almost seems to have become a moral mantra among pure-bred breeders. The insinuation of course is that it is dishonest, inhumane or worse to make money from a dog business! This is America, folks, and making money does not make you a bad breeder. One can combine excellence and profit!

On the subject of food, some dog food companies have a special program for breeders whereby the breeder gets big discounts on the cost of food. Such a program is good for the company, good for the breeders and, of course, good for the

Code of Ethics

These policies set forth breeding standards and outline the ethical behavior expected of member breeders. Breeder(s) signatures at the bottom of this statement reflect their agreement to abide by the Code of Ethics set forth herein and to welcome site visits and inspection of the premises and records.

dogs. Let's face it, the vast majority of puppy buyers are going to keep the pup on the same food anyway. Following is a general account of how these programs work: the company sends you puppy packets with food, pamphlets and coupons; you are required to give client addresses to the food manufacturer so that it can send your puppy-buyers first birthday cards for their puppies. The card includes a coupon for a free bag of food, thus encouraging people to keep using their brand. And you get most of your dog food almost free.

The new breeder will want to familiarize himself with and ascribe to the Breeder Code of Ethics recommended by the CCA. Breeders who do so and fill out a breeder form will receive free advertisement by the CCA. The CCA also grades breeders using a star rating method. The more stars, the better the breeder. Following is the CCA's Breeder Code of Ethics:

BREEDERS AGREE TO

1. Truthfully represent the quality of their dogs and to refrain from any deceptive advertising and/or maligning of their competition by making false or misleading statements about a person or their dogs.
2. Be fluent with and breed with the Standards in mind.
3. Refrain from selling puppies to pet stores, commercial brokers or dealers, puppy mills or to offer any as door or raffle prizes.
4. Be willing to take back any dog they have bred, for any reason, in their lifetime (or make suitable arrangements), rather than see it placed in a shelter.
5. Keep all dogs under clean and sanitary conditions, including housing appropriate for the climate, adequately sized run areas and encourage temperamental soundness and well being through regular daily personal contact.
6. Provide a system of identifying each dog (if over ten dogs) by collar and tags, tattooing or microchipping. Males must be kept separate from females so that there is no chance of breeding errors. Meticulous records must be kept. Dogs and business should be properly licensed in accordance with the laws of the community.
7. Provide a high quality diet and promote optimal health through regular worming, inoculations and periodic veterinary checks.
8. Maintain a minimum standard of yearly eye checks by a certified veterinary ophthalmologist (CERF) as required to

A lovely well-bred Cockapoo makes a priceless companion for life.

prevent the host of heritable eye defects so common in the parent breeds. Breeders who, in addition, elect to have vet checks done for hips, elbows and patellar abnormalities demonstrate that they have made every effort that their dogs are healthy and will have special recognition from the CCA.

9. Breed a limited number (less than five) breeds at one time.

10. Be a mentor and help breeders with less experience, remembering that once, we were all novices also.

11. Breed only non-related pairs of the healthiest, best tempered dogs.

12. Breed only dogs who have reached one year of age and until they are eight years. Over eight years, veterinary checks are recommended prior to breeding.

13. Breed only one stud dog to one female during a season. Should a second stud breed unintentionally, the pups must be sold without registration papers.

14. Consider a semi-annual test for *Brucella* on their breeding stock.

15. Breed only dogs who are CCA registered (N/A at present).

16. Have a written, dated and signed contract for outside stud services between the owner(s) of the male and the female which details type of remuneration expected.

A Breeding Program

Establish goals using your knowledge of genetics to breed pups that are closer to the standard than their parents. The stud and dam should complement each other and, if you are lucky, the pups, or some of them, will get the best qualities of each. This is where record-keeping comes in. By examining breeding records and the results, you will know what to do the next time.

A winning trio—
three of a kind!

SALES AND MARKETING

1. Carefully screen all potential buyers, educating them and making sure that they can provide suitable homes for a Cockapoo. Ensure that they know about the lifetime commitment of love, caring and funds necessary to properly have a dog as part of their family.

2. Be clear about and truthfully represent the qualities and deficits of the "breed."

3. Provide the new owner with a copy of the sales and warranty contract (CCA sample available) before pickup if possible.

4. Spay or neuter any dog with a genetic defect. Sell only as young pups with a spay or neuter agreement by withholding registration papers until the owner presents evidence that this has been done (N/A at present time). Spay or neuter retirees before placing them in homes.

5. Refrain from letting puppies go to new homes before six weeks of age, preferably seven. Only ship pups that are at least 10 weeks old because of the fear period between 8 and 10 weeks.

6. Give the new owners written instructions (see CCA sample puppy instructions) on the care of the pup, along with a sample of food if needed, and a record of worming and shots.

7. Use sales or special contracts to cover any other agreements made between breeder and owner.

8. Actively encourage the owners to contact the breeder for questions, comments or problems. A formalized system of litter follow-up is encouraged, such as using the Owner Survey on the CCA website.

Birds do it . . . even fuzzy
Cockapoos do it!

ESTABLISHING A BUSINESS

In addition to registering your kennel and keeping accurate accounting records, you will need to establish a list of charges for puppies, boarding, etc., and rules for a waiting list. Decide whether deposits are required, whether they're refundable and under what conditions. Your integrity is paramount here, and it will make or break you. Do remember that positive public relations are the best asset a business can have. Always be willing to negotiate to solve a problem. Usually, good breeders are in a position of not having enough supply to meet the demand, so a waiting list is a necessity. The author always had a waiting list of 60–100 pre-selected buyers who were required to make a $100 non-refundable deposit. One must maintain absolute list integrity as people will try to bribe you to advance to the top of the list. And the breeder must be flexible and compassionate when someone changes his mind and requests a refund. Always give the benefit of the doubt to the client. You don't want even one person out there bad-mouthing you.

PUPPY PARENTS AND THE SALE

Selection of homes for your pups is a somewhat complex process that starts with the first phone or email inquiry. Start off by asking about the prospective buyer's familiarity with Cockapoos. If you ask open-ended questions, it will encourage the inquirer to talk and reveal both his experience with Cockapoos and his history of dog ownership. By listening and prompting, you can find out a lot about a person. Ask about his family constellation, ages of children and experience with dogs. Are there other pets in the family? All this will give you an idea about what the buyer needs to know about you, your operation and your dogs. This initial contact is a good time to get an address and offer to send him a brochure. The brochure is an excellent sales tool and full-color brochures are available from the CCA. Ask the person to call you back after he receives the brochure and make an appointment to come and visit you and meet your adult dogs. This first contact is an excellent opportunity to educate, whether the person buys from you or not.

You also can get a good idea about whether he would be a suitable buyer or not. If his tone or what he says raises your hackles, it's advisable to end the conversation right then. Don't make excuses or lie, just say as nicely as you can that you do not believe that one of your dogs would be suitable for him. I once had a caller who wanted to keep the dog outdoors all the time. I just told him "not with one of my dogs."

The visit is a further opportunity to assess the suitability of the person or family to adopt one of your dogs. Observe whether all members of the family want a dog or not. You do not want to sell if one member of a couple wants a dog and the other doesn't. The poor dog will wind up in the middle. People often ask me "what do you say?" because they are so afraid of hurting someone's feelings. You don't have to be nasty or unpleasant, just say that perhaps another type of dog would be more suitable or you recommend waiting until the children are older. If you, the breeder, have done a good preliminary interview, it would be a rare circumstance for you to have the wrong kind of people visiting. This method is more time-consuming but well worth the effort for the peace of mind you will have when your pups go to their new homes.

Buyers who want one of your pups should be given a copy of the sales contract and puppy instructions along with a receipt for their deposit. There is way too much excitement when they come back to pick up their puppy to handle much but signing the contract and providing last-minute information and food. And what if something happens and they have to back out of the deal? If they want their deposit back, negotiate politely, as most people will be content to get a portion back. Then you create a win-win situation, as everyone is happy and you have created good PR.

It is a good idea to follow up a few days after the sale with a phone call to find out how the pup is adjusting and offer any support to the new "parents." This follow-up contact will reiterate your interest in the pup and encourage people to call you back. It is a good idea, even if you have not registered the litter with a registry, to give the family some kind of a pedigree certificate for their pup showing at least three generations, preferably five.

Adopting a Cockapoo should always be a win-win situation.

Are you ready to take on the responsibilit

Details of Cockapoo Breeding

Before the mating takes place, an agreement has to be reached between the owner of the stud and that of the female. And it should be in writing. A sample of a stud contract is on the CCA website. Usually the owner of the stud will take a "pick of the litter" or the money equivalent to the value of the top puppy. A proven stud's owner may ask for money at the time of mating, guaranteeing a return breeding if no pregnancy results. This is not the best deal to make as I have seen proven studs turn sterile for unknown reasons.

The female goes into season usually twice a year, each heat lasting three weeks. In the first week, there is swelling of the genitals and bleeding. Some females only swell and there is little or no blood. During the second week, the blood turns pinkish and she begins to "flag." Flagging means that she stands in such a way as to lift her tail and her genitals up for inspection to you, the family cat or the lamppost. It is an unmistakable departure from her normal behavior. She will flirt with anything, particularly a male dog, neutered or not. Having a male around, even a neutered one, is the best way to tell when she is ready. She will flirt and fling herself at him shamelessly. Do remember that neutered dogs can still mate. (The vet did not cut out his brain.) This middle week is when she is receptive to a male and the time

of becoming a Cockapoo breeder?

First-generation twin "Poos."

frame in which she should be bred. She will ovulate throughout this part of her cycle. Sperm deposited at this point can fertilize eggs that are two days old and will remain to fertilize the eggs that come along in the next two days. What this means is that it is only necessary to repeat the breeding every four days; that means day one, day four and day seven or eight. By that time, the female is usually into the final week of estrus and no longer receptive to the male. The old rule of thumb was to breed every other day and there is nothing wrong with doing it this way, especially if there is doubt as to the first day of the receptive cycle. Allowing a male to breed more than once in 48 hours is unwise as his sperm count can be lowered by over-breeding. With all these rules, believe it or not, there are exceptions. Females have been known to accept a male when they are not even in heat.

Traditionally, the female goes to the male to be bred, as there is some concern that the male might not perform out of his own territory. If this is the female's first experience, try to find an experienced stud and vice versa. Once it has been determined that the female is receptive and "standing" for the male, the female should be held, as it is much easier to hit a still target than a moving one. If there is a disparity in sizes, a "ladder" may have to be built. Phone books or couch cushions covered with a non-slip fabric work well.

After a short "get acquainted" period, the female should be held. One reason for holding the female is that each bitch reacts differently after the male inserts his penis. The male's penis has a bone in it that helps him to penetrate. Once he has penetrated, the penis

Two handfuls of two-day-old puppies.

Let sleeping "Poos" lie.

When Natural is not Possible

In some instances artificial insemination (AI) can be used when natural breeding is not possible. Fresh or frozen sperm can be used. The AKC has strict guidelines about AI, both fresh and frozen, so it is best to follow these. Even though Cockapoos are far from being an AKC breed, the AKC has much to offer in the way of educational material. AI is something best left to the vet to do and is not nearly as successful as natural breeding.

and glands swells up enough so that it won't come out, thus resulting in a "tie." There is also a pumping action to assure the maximum ejaculation of sperm. At this point the female may be very blasé or she may be writhing in agony and screaming her lungs out. If the latter, you need to hold her securely so that she does not hurt the male. Not only can he get bruised and sore, he can get the bone broken and that would be the end of his stud days.

The tie will last anywhere from a few minutes to an hour. Usually the male will turn around by lifting his leg over the bitch's rear end, and both of them will settle down to wait. When they separate, the dogs will lick themselves. This is very important for the male. His engorged penis should revert to normal size within an hour and retract into the sheath. Be sure to check him to make sure this has happened. If it has not, sometimes wet cold packs will help reduce the swelling; if it

does not retract within a short while, this is a veterinary emergency.

The female should be kept quiet for a while to assure that the sperm stay in her vagina and swim where they ought to! If more than an hour has elapsed and the tie is not broken, a cold pack applied to the male's testicles may help. Never ever try to force the issue.

The due date for the female is determined by counting 63 days from the date of first mating. Before you ever breed your female, move ahead two months on the calendar to make sure that you will be available for the delivery. And it would be a good idea to take her to the vet for a *Brucella* exam and general checkup. If receptive dates are in question, the vet can do a vaginal smear. Most authorities recommend not breeding before the age of 20 months, especially for larger dogs who mature more slowly than smaller ones. Some say not to start until the second heat. If the dog came in heat

A silver phantom puppy unmasked.

at six months and you followed the latter advice, you would be breeding her at one year.

How do you know when to retire your breeding stock? They will start having fewer puppies and you can figure that their eggs are running out. So you can expect to get about four good years of breeding from your female. The male can carry on and on. My little Hercules, who weighs in at 4.5 pounds and is a ninth-generation Cockapoo, is 15 now, blind and deaf, but a year ago he studded two females. I must admit that he needed a little help to "stay in" as getting the needed erection to effect a tie seemed to take longer. In all, he has produced 70 progeny with females from 5–15 pounds. He always produced at least one teacup toy in a litter, the smallest only going to 2 pounds adult weight. Is he king of all he surveys in my house? You bet! And he can still keep up on long walks! Hercules is a rare exception to the rule about a home breeder not keeping her own stud.

An Old Wives' Tale in the Dog Fancy

The female should only be bred once a year. Some go to such extremes that their female's reproductive cycle encompasses about two or three litters total in her lifetime. There is no scientific evidence to support this overly conservative approach. But the attitude is pervasive in the dog fancy, and you may be broadly criticized if you breed more than once a year. Keep in mind that the female has only a limited number of eggs, and these usually run out by age seven or so, whether you breed her or not. Back in the mid-1990s, Cornell University's *DogWatch* magazine had an article about breeding intervals. They found no reason that a healthy, parasite-free, well-nourished female could not be bred every cycle. They did, however, recommend a vet check before doing so. The main concern is whether the mother has fully recuperated from the last delivery and nursing. Nursing mothers almost always lose coat, and assessing coat condition is one of the best ways to determine whether she is ready to be bred again. I found that if the bitch had a large litter (five or six pups is a large litter for Cockapoos), she did not come in heat again until she was ready, and sometimes that was nine or ten months later. Good old Mother Nature provides! Most females are devoted mothers, but a few are not, and they should not be bred again. Some will cannibalize their offspring, but I have never seen that happen in my Cockapoos. Some "hop to" at the least sign of a baby crying and run back to the box; others take their good old time and let the babies yell.

TEA TIME FOR MOM
During pregnancy, be sure the dog gets plenty of her accustomed exercise. Strong muscles help to assure a normal whelping. Some people recommend giving raspberry leaf tea in the last two or three weeks of pregnancy. Raspberry leaf tea is a uterine tonic. Dogs simply do not have good tea-time manners, so mix a teaspoon or so of dry leaves with food or peanut butter.

PREGNANCY

Some dogs have false pregnancies (pseudocyesis), whether they have been bred or not. It is most common in dogs that have had a heat period and have not been bred. For most, it means some breast enlargement and some nesting behavior for a few weeks, but some actually go into labor. If symptoms last more than a month or are extreme, the dog should be taken to the vet.

There can be various reasons why a bitch fails to deliver healthy pups; sometimes puppies are reabsorbed by the mother and sometimes they are mummified. These cases may account for why your female does not "get pregnant." If you are expert at abdominal palpation, you may be able to feel embryos at three to four weeks of gestation.

Each female will respond differently to the hormones of pregnancy. Some have behavioral changes and become overly affectionate, wanting to be on your lap or next to you all the time. If you want to spend the money, you can have the vet do x-rays or a sonogram; otherwise, wait until she "shows." Most females will have some change in the nipples by three weeks. Some will keep you guessing until the last couple of weeks. If your female starts shivering and shaking in the early stages of pregnancy, she may have gas. My "Patches" did this every time she got pregnant, and multiple trips to the vet, examinations for vaginal/uterine infections and needless antibiotics did not help. Then one day a friend of mine who is a retired vet stopped to visit and said, "That dog has gas." She told me to get some human baby colic drops in the drugstore and give a few drops to Patches. Presto, the dog stopped shaking. It is all due to the hormonal changes of pregnancy.

Feed the dam as usual until the last couple of weeks.

Then it is a good idea to switch back to puppy food and increase the amount. Be careful that you do not allow her to get too fat. After delivery, free-feed her all the puppy chow she wants while she is actively nursing. Again, give no supplements or vitamins except oil for the coat.

Starting about a week before the due date, start tracking your dog's rectal temperature morning and night. The normal dog temperature is about 101.5°F. When there is a sudden drop in the temperature, say down to 99°F, you know that labor is imminent. This is usually a pretty reliable indicator, but not always. The dog can deliver up to a week before or after the due date.

Cockapoos and Cockers are known to be easy whelpers. If it is your female's first litter, she may act surprised when the first pup comes and seem not to know what to do. But after that, Mother Nature usually steps in and instinct takes over.

LABOR AND DELIVERY
Certain equipment is needed just in case: a crate with the top removed makes a good whelping box. Put old towels or sheets on the bottom and plenty of stuff for mama to knock around while nesting. Certain equipment will be needed if you choose to deliver the puppies yourself, including plenty of towels, blunt scissors and dental floss should you have to cut a cord, styptic powder to stop blood flow, a bulb syringe to suck mucus out of a newborn's mouth, lots of soft paper towels, Betadine antiseptic for the cords and a small box with heating pad under it to serve as an incubator for the newborns while mother is delivering others. Also keep on hand a food scale to weigh the newborns and a pad and pen to record time of birth, sex, color and identifying marks. Red nail polish can be used to identify puppies of the same

Keeping Records

You may think that recording time of birth is silly, but I was surprised at how many people wanted to run horoscopes on their puppies!

sex who look exactly alike. For example, black female A is identified by red nail polish on her left hind toes, black female B by her right hind toes. The dab of nail polish will stay on a long time. Rickrack or string does not.

Most females seem to start labor by shivering, panting, being generally restless and rearranging the bedding in the whelping box *ad infinitum*. This may go on for 24 hours or more until the second stage of labor begins. This is when her sides start heaving and she pushes. Check her genital area every so often to see if there are signs of a puppy forthcoming. It will appear as the amniotic sac bulging out of the vagina with perhaps a dark or light mass inside. (This is the point at which you may want to remove towels and replace them with disposable incontinence pads.) You may be able to make out a little foot or two. Keep mom and the room

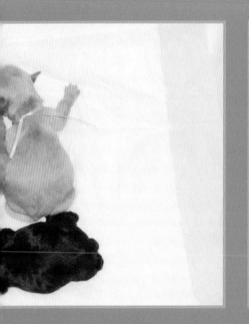

On the third day, the pups rested.

Day four.
The pups sleeping on
their littermates.

quiet with only people she knows "assisting." Do not let other pets near her as curious as they will be. Talk to mom calmly and encourage her. Offer her a little broth if you like. She probably will not eat or drink.

Most literature recommends that you call the vet if mom has been in hard labor for more than two hours with no pup or if labor stops (uterine inertia). You should not have to do much during delivery as the mother will use her teeth to break the sac and lick the pup to stimulate breathing. She will then start to eat the placenta use her back teeth to crush and sever the umbilical cord. When the mother starts to chew the umbilical cord, hold the pup and about an inch of the cord between you and mom to prevent her from chewing the cord too short. I have always done this and never been bitten, nor have I ever had the mother chew the cord too close. Put a little Betadine on the cord to prevent infection and let it dry before returning the pup to the mother. She does a much better job than we could ever do, so don't rush to help when help is not needed. The only time to help is if the puppies are coming too fast. You may break the sac, suck out the nose and mouth with the bulb syringe and rub the baby with a terrycloth towel. If the baby seems to be congested or breathing with difficulty, grab him securely, head down, with a towel and swing him in a down arc. This will help fluids to drain out of the mouth or nose. The pup can then be put in the "incubator" while mom is concentrating on the next one. She may get very upset when you do this and the better part of valor may be to put the pup back with her. Do make sure that a placenta accompanies each puppy.

Knowing when she has finished delivering is an art and a science. Feel for more pups in the abdomen and you should get an "empty" feeling. Even then, you can't always be sure what you are feeling. It is easy to mistake the cecum or a kidney for a puppy. Take the mother out in the yard on a leash and walk her around and let her relieve herself. Be prepared with a towel in case she drops a puppy in the yard. She will spend the entire time pulling you back to the nursery. I always carried mine to the extreme perimeter of the yard and hoped they relieved themselves as they pulled me back.

So now, clean up the bedding, offer mom breakfast in bed and plenty of fresh water, put the top on the crate and let mom have a well-deserved rest. All the puppies ought to have found a nipple. For the next two or three weeks, there should be very little to do except keep the bedding clean, take care of mom and see that puppy dewclaws are removed in the first five days. Do not dock tails. It is painful and has no redeeming value. A dog uses its tail for balance and expression. After 24 hours, all pups should be suckling well and have nice round little bellies pooching out at the sides. You can weigh them daily but the "poochy belly" tells the tale. Mother will bleed for several days to a week or more, but not to worry unless it is a copious amount. Keep a check on mother's breasts and look for lumps, hot areas and scratches from the puppies' nails. You will need to start clipping toenails soon after birth. Be cautious about where the mother goes and what toxins she could bring into her puppies such as insecticides from the grass or salt from the streets if you live in a cold climate. If these conditions exist, wash the mom's feet and breasts.

A mother with only one or two pups usually has a more difficult delivery and will likely need a Caesarian section. It is not good for a puppy to be raised alone as he misses out on all the lessons he is supposed to learn from his littermates. If this does happen and there are other mothers with multiple births, take a puppy from one and give him to the singleton mother. I remember this happening with

SPECIAL PUPPY CARE

Once in a while a particular mother's puppies seem to suffer from colic. They are very noisy pups and cry all the time although they are eating and gaining weight. Others are quiet as church mice and just as small too! As with human babies, they stop crying when you pick them up and rub their little bellies. The crying does not seem to bother mama dog at all. And sometimes there will be a puppy that does not thrive and seems to need extra attention. Perhaps he is not as strong or big as his brawny brothers and gets last choice of dinner stations. Tube- or bottle-feeding formula is not a good idea as the pup usually dies of aspiration pneumonia. Instead, pick mother up in your lap and allow the pup first chance to feed at all the best nipples. Sometimes a little favoritism is all he will need.

Let the fun begin! The gang of five
at a few weeks of age.

Suzie and her brood content in her crate.

my little "Brandy" who weighed all of 5 pounds when I first started breeding. "Suzie," a larger Cockapoo, had delivered a litter of six. Brandy kept on jumping out of her crate, running over to Suzie's and telling me "I want one of those babies" as plain as plain can be. So when Suzie had her back turned, I took one of her babies, washed it up and smeared it with Brandy's vaginal discharge and Brandy immediately adopted it as one of her own and settled down. Lucky for me, dogs cannot count and Suzie never knew she was missing a puppy. Who knows, perhaps Suzie and Brandy made a doggie agreement!

We all want every puppy to live, but sometimes it is best to let nature take its course. I do not advocate extreme measures to keep a fading or gasping puppy alive as more than likely there is something wrong that we cannot see. Maternal rejection, especially from an experienced dam, also probably indicates an unseen defect.

Mother's Day is
some "dam" holiday.

PUPPY RAISING

The puppies' eyes open at around two weeks of age and now the fun begins! Turn the crate bottom opening toward a wall so they cannot wander out and get lost. Now is the time to put them in the whelping box you have prepared.

Some breeders use those child's plastic wading pools but the material is too slippery and not good for leg development. Professional-type whelping boxes can be lovely and are equipped with a side railing that is supposed to prevent the mother from leaning against the side of the box and crushing a puppy. I say "supposedly" as I never had that happen. Mama dogs are very careful and are amazing in the way they nose all the

Nothing is as rewarding as bringing a smiling,
loving Cockapoo home. Just ask the family cat!

puppies into the middle of the crate and lie down with them but not on them. I never had any mishaps although other breeders swear they have. I think a lot of unexplained puppy deaths are attributed to the mother "sitting on them" when they were just supposed to die anyway. Or perhaps Cockapoos are too smart to sit on their own offspring.

A great whelping box can be made if a person is just a little handy with tools. I cut up a sheet of plywood into equal heights, painted them with enamel paint and fastened them together with door hinges on the outside. Be careful not to have anything on the inside that could injure a puppy. You want the sides high enough so the puppies will not be able to get out when they get bigger, but short enough for mama to jump in and out.

Another advantage to the hinges is that the pin can be pulled out when the enclosure is no longer needed and the sections stored flat for the next time. (Be sure to number the hinge parts before you take it apart.)

Something waterproof, like one of those blue tarps, needs to go under the enclosure to protect your flooring or carpeting. On top of that, you need some kind of material for the pups to walk on. I experimented with all kinds of material for the floor, including lugging in sod, the concept being if pups did their business only on grass for weeks, they would then just naturally take to going only on grass. Fifteen trips to the massage therapist later, it proved to be a dismal failure. The sod got real smelly very fast and had to be changed often. The best solution was incontinence pads (nice and disposable) for the pups to walk on until they started ripping those up. I then switched to rubber mats made with non-slip material. These were fairly easily washed with the hose in the back yard and were great for the puppies' leg development. I like to keep

LITTER BED BUGS

Puppies require a lot of the breeder's time as they mature. Mother dog may do most of the care and feeding for the first few weeks, but once they get their teeth, she's going to say to the breeder, "They're all yours."

Hours will be spent picking up the papers or changing the litter tray, as well as making certain that the puppies have plenty of fresh water and are fed on a schedule four times per day. Their whelping box must be kept clean and sanitary to prevent disease and infection, since puppies are susceptible to bacterial and viral infections as their immune systems are still weak.

At the age of four weeks, the puppies will be crawling around and trying to work their way out of the whelping box. At five weeks, they'll need to have space to run and play as their exercise requirements increase. When the puppies are five weeks of age, they'll need to have their first worming treatment. At seven weeks, it's time for the second worming and the first round of shots.

It's not easy being mom to a litter of puppies!

the crate in these enclosures so that puppies remained accustomed to using the crate as a bed. It is also fun to have more than one litter of pups in the same enclosure. The moms take turns nursing them all, sometimes with the cutest pained expressions on their faces as all these pups are hanging off them. The moms need to be watched as one may not do her part and leave most of the work to the "Supermom."

The first thing puppies do after opening their eyes is to start exploring their environment, each other and toys. They start to naturally extend their paws into space. This is the cutest little gesture, and at this point it is really easy to teach them to shake hands while you are playing with them. All my puppies went to their new homes knowing how to "shake hands." Puppies should be played with as often as possible, at least once a day. A word of caution: make sure that all children sit down on the floor to play with the puppies. Children can and do easily drop pups. At least if seated on the floor, the pups cannot fall far. Of course, one has to keep reminding the children to stay seated, and supervise them closely.

At about the age of four weeks, the pups can begin to learn to eat. This is a fun time, and the handiest item to use for food is an angel-food cake tin. The construction prevents a lot of the "walking through the food dish" behavior. Use mom's kibble soaked in hot water. The babies will have to be encouraged to eat at first, usually by putting a little mush into their mouths, but they catch on very quickly. Keep mom away or she will eat all their food. You can let her clean the plate when

they are finished.

As soon as you start feeding the pups, mother stops cleaning up after them and that becomes your job! And they are little poop machines. If you aren't fastidious in picking up after them, they will walk through it, get it all over them and create a big mess. As they eat better and better, mom will nurse less and less often. Usually pups are pretty well weaned by six weeks, but some of the more devoted mothers will let her pups nurse until they are a couple of months old. As soon as pups have teeth to chew with, you can stop soaking the food and just feed them dry, small-bite kibble. Your water bowl should be heavy so that the toddlers can't knock it over, but not so big that a pup could swim in it and drown. Rest assured, they will walk through it, lie in it and knock it over if they can.

INDEX